Julius Gay

A Record of the Descendants of John Clark, of Farminton, Conn

Conn

The Male Branches Brought Down to 1882. The Female Branches...

Julius Gay

A Record of the Descendants of John Clark, of Farminton, Conn
The Male Branches Brought Down to 1882. The Female Branches...

ISBN/EAN: 9783337142681

Printed in Europe, USA, Canada, Australia, Japan

Cover: Foto ©ninafisch / pixelio.de

More available books at **www.hansebooks.com**

The Clark House in Farmington.

Built by John Clark, about 1700. Pulled down 1880.

A

RECORD OF THE DESCENDANTS

OF

JOHN CLARK,

OF

FARMINGTON, CONN.

THE MALE BRANCHES BROUGHT DOWN TO 1882. THE
FEMALE BRANCHES ONE GENERATION AFTER THE
CLARK NAME IS LOST IN MARRIAGE.

By JULIUS GAY.

— — • — —

HARTFORD, CONN.:

PRESS OF THE CASE, LOCKWOOD & BRAINARD COMPANY.

1882.

PREFACE.

This genealogy of the descendants of John Clark of Farmington has been compiled at the request of Dennis Woodruff Clark, Esq., of Portland, Maine, a descendant of the sixth generation. I have aimed to copy all dates from contemporary records, but whenever I have been obliged to rely on more recent testimony, or when authorities differ, I have given my authority. In collecting the very few scattered records of the early members of the family from old bibles and wills, and moss-covered gravestones, I have been constantly reminded of that valley of dry bones in Holy Writ in which the prophet was asked " Can these dry bones live?" Doubtless the reader will find the fragments dry enough and lifeless enough, but if he finds little but a carefully joined skeleton, it shall not be built up of " unrelated parts," such as critics claim to find in some now famous statues. Here, at the outset, we meet the great difficulty of the work. The family of Clark, or Clerk as the name was often spelled, was a numerous one, as are most of those named from occupations, such as Smith, Cook, Miller, Porter, and numerous others. John was one of the most common of Christian names, so that it is not wonderful that almost every old New England town had a John Clark among its early settlers.

The descendants of John Clark of Farmington believe that he was identical with John of Cambridge, Mass., and with John of Hartford, and this is set down as an ascertained fact by Rev. Wm. S. Porter, a genealogist of great industry and local research. The Clarks of Saybrook, Ct., claim that John of Cambridge, of Hartford, and of Saybrook, were identical, and quote the authority of Hinman. No contemporaneous record has been found to confirm or subvert either theory. I shall follow the advice of that veteran genealogist, D. Williams Patterson, Esq., of Newark Valley, N. Y., and state the prominent facts known regarding each of these men in the hope that they may be found so related to other facts possibly hereafter discovered as to help determine which theory is true.

JULIUS GAY.

FARMINGTON, CONN., Sept., 1882.

EARLY SETTLERS NAMED JOHN CLARK.

JOHN CLARK OF CAMBRIDGE.

John Clerke, as the name is spelled, took the freeman's oath at the General Court held Nov. 6, 1632. He was one of the forty-two men to whom land was assigned at Newtown, now Cambridge, on the 29th of March, 1632.* "An agreement by the inhabitants of the New Town, about paling in the neck of land. Imprimis, That every one who hath any part therein shall hereafter keep the same in good and sufficient repair; and if it happen to have any defect, he shall mend the same within three days after notice given, or else pay ten shillings a rod for every rod so repaired for him. Further, It is agreed that the said impaled ground shall be divided according to every man's proportion in said pales." His share in the paling was three rods in an aggregate of 577. Who these forty-two men were in part appears in a statement by Winthrop.† "The Braintree company, (which had begun to sit down at Mount Wollaston,) by order of court, removed to Newtown. These were Mr. Hooker's company." Others of them came afterward. John Haynes, subsequently Governor of Massachusetts and later of Connecticut, whose name heads the list, did not arrive until Sept. 4, 1633,‡ so that the division may have been made at a still later date. In his

* History of Cambridge, by Lucius R Paige, p. 10.
† Savage's Winthrop, i, 104.
‡ Ibid., i, 130.

History of Cambridge, p. 510, Paige states that John Clark
" owned the lot on the easterly corner of Brattle and Mason
streets in 1635, which he sold to Edward Winship, and
removed to Hartford." A description of his lands in Newtown is given in the following verbatim copy from page 84 of
" The Regestere Booke of the Lands and Howses in the New-
towne. 1635." " Edward Winchep bought of John Clarke
one house, with two Acres of ground, upon the Cowe Common, Guy Bainbridge North, Cowe Common East, the high
waye to Watertown west, the way betweene Watertowne and
Charlstown north, Mrs. Glouer South.

John Clarke In West End About [   ] Ackrs John
Haynes Esqr. one the son [   ] the Common one the North
East, Guy Bainbrigg one the North west, the High [   ] to
Water Towne one the south west.

Moore in Cow yard Rowe About one [   ] Cow yard lane
north east, Daniell Pat [   ] south east, Brayntre street highway [   ] south west, John White North west.

Moore In Ould ffeild aboute one acker [   ] one roode
Edward Elmer North west, [   ] Comon pale one North east,
William Lewis one the south east, the highway to [   ] oyster
bancke one the south west.

Moore one Smale lott hill Aboute Three Ackers William
Spencer North east [   ] Samuel Dudly south east, Garrand
[   ] south west , Highway to Comon Pales north west.

Moore in the Great Marsh about th [   ] Ackers Nathaniell
Richards north west, Charles River south west, Samuel Dudly
south east, Andrew Warner North east."

The following entry* appears on the Town Records under
date March 1, 1635–6:

* History of Cambridge, by Lucius R. Paige, p. 38.

"Agreed with John Clarke to make a sufficient wier to catch alewives upon Menotomies River in the bounds of this town, before the 12th of April next, and shall sell and deliver unto the inhabitants of the town and no other, except for bait, all the alewives he shall take at iii^s., 6^d. per thousand, and shall at all times give such notice to the persons that shall be appointed to fetch them away as he shall be directed, who shall discharge the said John Clarke of them within 24 hours after notice, or else he to have liberty to sell them to whom he can. Provided, and it is the meaning of the Townsmen, that if any shall desire to have some to eat before the great quantity cometh, then he is to have ii^d. a score and fetch them there, or iii^d. a score and he bring them home. Further the Townsmen do promise in the behalf of the town to make good all those fish that he shall be damnified by the Indians, that is, shall himself deliver unto them, being appointed before by the Townsmen how many he shall deliver. Also to save him harmless from any damage he shall sustain by Wattertowne, provided it be not his own fault. He is to have his money within 14 days after he hath done fishing."

April 4, 1636. "Andrew Warner and Joseph Cooke to make a rate for the division of the alewives."

April 23, 1636. "Agreed with Andrew Warner to fetch home the alewives from the weir: and he is to have xvi^d. a thousand and load them himself, for carriage ; and to have power to take any man to help him, he paying him for his work.

" Andrew Warner appointed to see a cartway made to the weir."

This is the last record I find of him in Newtown.

JOHN CLARK OF HARTFORD.

He was a soldier in the Pequot fight and must have been in Hartford as early as 1637. On the first day of May, 1637, the General Court at Hartford "ordered that there shall be an offensive war against the Pequoitt." After the return of the soldiers from their successful campaign, a tract of land containing from sixty to eighty acres, long known as *Soldiers Field*, was divided among them. John Clark was an owner of land in this tract, and therefore presumably one of the soldiers in the Pequot fight. On the 9th of March, 1641, the town ordered Matthew Marvin to maintain a fence . . . . " to the corner of John Clark's lot lying in the soldiers field."*

Also land is recorded as owned by Zachariah Field, June 9, 1659, viz., " one parcel lying in the Soldier's Field which he bought of John Clark containing by estimation one Rood."

At a General Meeting of the town held the 14th of January 1639, it was voted " Whereas there is some difference in allotments, some having more than is according to their due proportion, it is therefore ordered that Mr. Hopkins, Mr. Wells, Mr. Warner, John Pratt, Timothy Standly, John Clark, Joseph Mygatt . . . . shall examine the same and shall have power to appoint every mans portion according as in their judgment shall be just and equal."

I find no record of any deeds of land executed by John Clark. It was the early custom in Hartford and other towns to record a description of all the pieces of land owned by each man in one place in the record, but not to record deeds of conveyance at length. The record of John Clark's land begins as follows—

* See also Hartford in the Olden Time, I. W. Stuart, p. 116.

" February Anno Dom. 1639.

Several parcels of land in Hartford upon the River of Connecticut belonging to John Clark & to his heirs forever. One parcel on which his dwelling house now standeth with yards or gardens therein being, that whereof lyeth in the West Field, containing by estimation four acres more or less, abutting upon the highway leading from Seth Grant's to the Sentinel Hill on the east, and Mr. Allen's land on the west, and on William Ruscoe's land and on William Parker's land on the south and on Thomas Burcharde's land on the north."

A description of eleven other pieces follows. The house and lot above described were sold by John Clark to Zachariah Field, as appears in the description of lands of the latter recorded January 1650. The house stood on what was known as the 38th lot of the 8th tier on the west side of the highway now known as Trumbull Street and very near the east line of Allyn Street. Its position is laid down on the map in I. W. Stuart's " Hartford in the Olden Time," and a further description may be found in Porter's " Historical Notices of Hartford," p. 23. Other references to John Clark appear on the town records of Hartford, as follows:

September 1639—" It is ordered that Goodman Scott, Goodman Clark and Goodman Ely shall reserve the common " . . . " and if Thomas Scott, John Clark and Goodman Ely fail of measuring within the time set, they shall forfeit five shillings."

General Meeting, Feb. 18, 1640—John Clark with eleven others on a committee to divide " the land on the east side of the Great River."

January 12, 1642—" There was chosen surveyors for the year, John Clark and John Wilcox."

2

John Clark probably removed from Hartford previously to
1655, for his name does not appear in the list of tax payers
in the "mill rates" for the years 1655, 1656, and 1657, which
are preserved. His name is however found in the lists of
"The proprietors of the undivided lands in Hartford with
such of their proportions in one division as followeth according to which proportions they paid for the purchase of the said
lands" in the years 1665, 1666, 1671, and 1672. These divisions of the "undivided lands" were however made to non-
residents and even to the heirs of deceased proprietors. In
the divisions of 1674 and 1682, his name ceases to appear.

A John Clark, whether the same, I know not, was a juror
at Hartford, Sept. 1641, and Oct. 1642, also a deputy, May,
1649. A John Clark also had ten children baptized in the
first church of Hartford in 1704–1724.

JOHN CLARK OF SAYBROOK.

John Clark of Saybrook was a man of note in the colony,
a patentee named in the Charter of King Charles II. in 1662,
for many years a deputy from Saybrook to the General Court,
and a man to whose executive ability were entrusted many
public commissions.

The earliest date I can find under which he is distinctly
named as of Saybrook, is that of September 9, 1647, when
"Captain Mason & Jo: Clark are desired to carry on the
building of the Fort, by hiring men or Cartts or other neces-
saryes. They are aloud to mak vse of the last Rate to be
paid by Seabrook." (*See Colonial Records of Conn.*)

His will is recorded in the Probate Records of New Haven,
in vol. i, part 2, page 50, and is dated February 17, 1672, at
the beginning, and January 19, 1673, at the end. It is also
printed at length in the *Pratt Genealogy*, page 340. His
inventory is dated February 28, 1673. He names—

" My son John Clark of Saybrook."

" My son William Pratt," that is, son-in-law.

" My daughter Elizabeth Pratt," who, it appears by the Pratt Genealogy, married William Pratt in June, 1636, he dying in 1678.

" My daughter Sarah Huntington."

" My wife's twenty pounds, which she is to have at my decease."

" Abigail Fletcher," daughter of his wife Mary.

He also had a son Joseph, whose will, recorded in Hartford Probate Records, vol. iii, page 7, is dated Milford, Aug. 27, 1658, " I being at this Instant Bownd upon a Voyadge to the West Indes." His inventory was taken Aug. 27, 1663.

After the death of her husband, the widow removed to Farmington and lived with her son-in-law, John Stanley. Here she died, Jan. 22, 1678. She has so often been erroneously supposed the wife of John Clark of Farmington, that it may be well to state that she was the daughter of the widow Joyce Ward of Wethersfield, previously of Rutland County, England, who died between Nov. 15, 1640, and Feb. 24, 1640–1, and left children, viz., Edward, Anthony, William, Robert, John, and Mary. Mary married before March 4, 1640–1, John Fletcher of Wethersfield, and had children—

i. Sarah, b. 1641; m. John Standly.

ii. Hannah, b. 1643; m. Dec. 12, 1665, John Chittenden, son of William.

iii. Elizabeth, baptized October, 1645; m. Elnathan Bockford.

iv. Samuel, b. 1649; d. young.

v. Abigail, baptized June 13, 1652.

vi. Mary, m. —— Stevens.

vii. Rebecca, m. Oct. 10, 1653, Andrew Warner of Hartford.

John Fletcher was admitted to the church in Milford,
Nov. 14, 1641, and Mary his wife, Dec. 19, 1641. John
Fletcher died April 18, 1662. See Trumbull's Colonial Rec-
ords of Connecticut, vol. i, page 451, Milford Town and
Church Records, and Savage's Dictionary.

JOHN CLARK OF FARMINGTON.

John Clark, the ancestor of the family whose genealogy is
hereafter recorded, was an early settler of Farmington, how
early does not appear. He had been a resident long enough
to have acquired numerous pieces of land when the town
registrar made a formal record of them in the month of
January, 1657. The names of John Clark and his wife
were included in a list of the members of the church in
Farmington made March 1, 1679–80. When they joined is
not stated. He was made a freeman in May, 1664. (See
Colonial Records, vol. i, pp. 412 and 427.) On the 27th of
December, 1682, he was chosen a Chimney Viewer by the
town, with the following instructions : " Att the saem meeting
it was vooted and agreed yᵗ the Chimney viewers should
atend their work of veiuing chimnyes & Ladders one in six
weeks in yᵉ winter and in yᵉ Sumer one a quarter and for
each neglect hear of they shall paye to yᵉ touen treshuer
tenn shillings."* On the 28th of December, 1685, and again
on the 8th of December, 1690, he was chosen a surveyor of
highways. What offices he may previously have held we
know not, since the formal record of town meetings begins

---

* The custom of paying them nothing for their services, but of fining
them for refusing to accept office and for every neglect of duty, must have
been about as satisfactory to the office holders of these good old times as
the decision attributed to Wouter Van Twiller, the renowned Governor
of New Amsterdam, who, after condemning the plaintiff and defendant
in a law-suit to give each other a receipt in full, ordered the constable to
pay the costs.—*Knickerbocker's History of New York.*

with that of Dec. 27, 1682. Some few entries there are of
an older date of matters thought of sufficient importance to
be "transcribed out of ye ould book," but no lists of town
officers.

His house stood on High Street, as will appear by a con-
sideration of the following extracts from the land records of
the town:

Vol. II, p. 84. "Jan. 1657 to John Clark

One ysell on which his dwelling house now standeth with
yeardes or orcherdes thearein being, contāin by estimā Ten
acres be it more or less y^t wheare of he bought of John Stell
& ded sum tyme belong to Robberd Willson. A butting on
porke brook on the East & on William Smith's land on the
West & on John Stell's land on the South and on the highway on the North."

Vol. I, p. 9. "Description of Lands of William Lewis
February 1665.

One ysell with a mesage or teniment thereon standing
orchard gardens therein being Containing by estimā two
icres 10 or 20 perches abutting on John Clark's Land to y^e
East & to ye West on a highway Leading to James Bird's for
his yticulor use and to ye South on James bird's land & to y^e
North on ye Common highway Leading to hartford which the
said William Lewis bought of John Clarke."

Vol. I, p. 24. "March 18, 1667. Land in Farmington,
in the Jurisdiction of Connecticut, belonging to John Clark
and his heirs forever—viz: one parcell on which his dwelling
house now standeth, with other houses and barns, gardens
therein being, containing by estimation seven acres, three
roods, twenty-eight perches, be it more or less, butting to the
North on Joseph Bird's land in part, and part on the highway
leading to Hartford; to the South on James Bird's land, and

to the East on Jonathan Smith's land, and to the West on
Benjamin Judd his land, that he bought of John Steele, Senior, that given him by the town."

Vol. I, p. 12. "Att a town meetinge in ffarmington, March
16, 1673. att the same meetinge there was Chosen for a Committy to Laye out A highway for the use of the Town, from
John Clark's and so cross the end of the Lotts to the highway
that runs up to the mountain by Abraham Andruses house:
serj. John Wadsworth, John Standly. junr, and Benjamin
Judd and John Clark."

This is the street known for many years on the records as
Back Lane, but now called High Street.

Vol. I, p. 12. To John Clark, Junior. "One parcel of
land on which his dwelling house and barn now standeth,
containing by estimation five roods, be it a little more or a
little less. being part of his father, John Clark, his house lot,
as appeareth by a deed dated the eighth of April, in the year
one thousand seven hundred and two. A butting eastward
and northward on his father, John Clark, his house lot, and
westward on a highway and southward on James Bird, Sen.,
his land."

It appears, then, that in 1657 John Clark owned 10 acres,
reaching eastward to Poke brook, and westward near to the
site of Cephas Skinner's (formerly Manin Curtis') house,
comprising about the same premises now owned by Charles
L. Whitman, John Riley, and Mrs. Barney; that in or before
1665 he sold 2½ acres from the western end to William
Lewis: that in 1667 he still owned the remainder. In 1673
High street was cut through the original ten-acre lot, and in
1702 John Clark gave to his son John five roods of land from
the southwest corner of his house lot. The house of John
Clark, Sen., must then have stood between the present (1882)

sites of the houses of John Riley and Mrs. Barney, and the
house of John Clark, Jun., must have been the old house
next south, pulled down in 1880. John Clark was the owner
of numerous pieces of land, by purchase, by the grant of the
town, and by the many divisions of the "Reserved Land"
among the eighty-four proprietors. His possessions were
scattered here and there northward to "a place cittuate
within the bounds of ffarmington att a place comonly called
and known by the name of Brownsons Nodd, and Lying
northward of said ffarmington on the west side of the great
River which runneth throw ffarmington meadowes, and is
nigh unto Simsbery bounds," to the south as far as the Great
Plain, and eastward and westward to the farthest boundaries
of the town.

This account of the place where he lived and the lands he
owned is about all we can gather concerning the ancestor of
a numerous race. Of his wife, or, more probably, wives,
who bore him as many children as blessed the patriarch
Jacob, we know not even the names, nor when or where they
were born or were married or died. An old family record,
taken down long since from the lips of an aged member of
the family, tells us that John Clark came from Scotland, and
that his wife was an English lady. The only other mention
I find of her is in the Record of the First Church in Farmington, wherein the Rev. Samuel Hooker enrolls John Clark
and *his wife* as members, on the first day of March, 1680.

The record of the will of John Clark is as follows:

"The Last Will and Testament of John Clark, late of
Farmington, Sen., deceased.

"In the name of God Amen. The last Will & Testament
of John Clark, Senr, of Farmington, in the County of Hartford and Colony of Connecticut, in New England, made this

Eighth day of Feb. in the year of our Lord One Thousand
Seven Hundred and nine—ten[*], as followeth, viz: The said
John Clark being at this time in good health and, through
the goodness of God, in the possession of my reason, for
which I desire to bless his holy name. But being grown into
age, so that I cannot expect the time of my departure out of
this life to be very far off, and not knowing how soon nor
how suddenly it may come upon me, am therefore desirous
accounting it my duty to do what I can to prevent trouble
among my surviving children that God shall graciously please
to continue after my decease, I do therefore make and ordain
this to be my last will and testament, and do desire my executor or executors, whom I shall in these presents nominate
and appoint, to see that this my will be performed when
there shall be occasion for it, after my decease.

1. I desire to commit myself soul and body to God as my
Great Creator and to Jesus Christ as my merciful Redeemer
through the merit of whose blood and perfect obedience I
hope to obtain salvation from the wrath which is to come;
and as for my body, I desire to commit it into the hands of my

---

[*] An explanation of this and numerous other instances of double dating
occurring in this book may be found convenient. The year in the old
style began with March 25th, called Lady Day. March was thus the first
month of the year, April the second, February the twelfth, etc. In 1583
Pope Gregory XIII. made the year begin with January 1st, and added ten
days to the reckoning by striking out October 5th to 14th, inclusive, from
the year 1582. Thus April 10th became April 20th. In England the
change was not made until January 1, 1752, eleven days being struck out
of the following month of September. September 3d to 13th, inclusive,
did not appear in the English Calendar for 1752. September 2d was Wednesday and September 14th was the following Thursday. From 1583 to
1752, to avoid ambiguity, double dating was introduced. February 8th, the
date of John Clark's will, 1709-10, or 17⁹⁄₁₀, as usually written, means
Wednesday, February 8, 1709, old style, or February 19, 1710, new style.
For further information see N. E. Historical & Genealogical Register, Vol.
XX. p. 40, or "Coburn's Almanacs for 3,000 Years," Boston, 1882.

christian friends and relations only to be decently interred in
the earth, which being done and all my just debts and funeral
expenses paid, then my will also is in the 2d place that my
son Matthew Clark shall have all my land both meadow and
uplands and all my outlands both divided and undivided as
also my house and barn and remainder of my homestead that
is not already disposed of in deeds of gift and also all my
moveable estate of what kind, sort or degree soever that I
shall stand possessed of at my death and not legally conveyed
away by me in my life time, he paying, or his heirs, executors
or administrators paying within one year after my decease, the
several legacies in these presents after mentioned—3ly I give
to my daughters that shall survive me to each one of them
five pounds to be paid by son Matthew or by his heirs executors or administrators within twelve months after my decease
in pay* and not in money—4ly and finally my will is that my
son Matthew Clark be and by these presents I do appoint
him to be whole and sole executor to this my last will and
testament, and I desire my two loving friends and kinsmen
John Hart Sen. and Deac. Samuel Porter to be overseers
hereof. In witness whereof and to every part hereof I the
said John Clark Sen. have on this day and year above named
both signed, sealed and declared this to be my last will and
testament.

JOHN CLARK Sen. his mark ʌ & seal (a seal.)

* Madam Sarah Knight, in her "Journal of a Horseback Journey from
Boston to New York, and Return," 1704, describes the currency of the
day as "Pay, Money, Pay as Money and Trusting. Pay is Grain, Pork,
Beef &c. at the prices set by the General Court that year. Money is Pieces
of Eight, Ryalls, or Boston or Bay shillings (as they call them,) or Good
hard money, as sometimes silver coin is termed by them, also Wampum,
viz. Indian beads which serves for change. Pay as Money is provisions
as aforesaid one-third cheaper than as the Assembly or General Court sets
it, and Trust as they and the merchant agree for time" . . . . "A six-
penny knife in pay is 12d—in pay as money 8d and hard money its own
price, viz. 6d."

3

Signed, sealed & declared in the presence of John Hart
sen. John Hart jun.

And as an addition to this my will I the said John Clark
Sen. do declare it to be my will that my youngest daughter
Mercy Clark not being disposed of in marriage and so not
having had anything as portion as the rest of my daughters
have had as also being by the providence [of God] under
greater disadvantages than the rest of them. That she shall
have after my decease all my moveable estate of household
goods forever. 2ly, I do further add that it is my will that
my daughter Rebecca Woodruff, with whom I am, be well
rewarded by my executor for all her labor, care and trouble
about me in this time of my sickness according to the judgment
of my two friends Dea— Samuel Porter and John Hart Sen.

In witness hereunto I have set my hand this 21st day of
November 1712.

JOHN CLARK Sen. ⋀ his mark.

In presence of John Hart Sen., John Hart Jun."

He died the next day and the town clerk made the entry,
" John Clark of ffarmington ye aged Departed his Natural
Life twenty-second of Novembr In ye year of or Lord 1712."

His children were :

2. i.   JOHN.
3. ii. MATTHEW.
4. iii. ELIZABETH.
5. iv. REBECCA.
6. v.   MARY, b. about 1667.
7. vi. SARAH.
8. vii. MARTHA.
9. viii. ABIGAIL.
10. ix. HANNAH, baptized April 4, 1680, " born a few days
         before."
11. x.   RACHEL.
    xi. MERCY.

There was also an Ebenezer Clark, son of John Clark, baptized August 10, 1690, who must have died young, since his name is not mentioned in the distribution of the estate of John Clark, Jr., April 9, 1712, unless he belonged to some other family, which is improbable.

2.

John[2] (*John*[1]) must have been born before 1673, for he was elected to the office of hayward Dec. 17, 1694, and on the same day received a grant of land from the town. He married Sarah Warner of Middletown, Conn., born March 6, 1669–70, daughter of Robert and Elizabeth (Grant) Warner. John died Oct. 6, 1709.

His widow *probably* married, October 25, 1711, Capt. Job Ellsworth, born April 13, 1674, son of Josias and Elizabeth (Holcomb) Ellsworth. Job died September 29, 1751, and Sarah was living September 5, 1750, when Job executed his will. (*See Stiles' History of Windsor*, 600.) John Clark was known as Sergeant John Clark. His house, shown in the frontispiece to this volume, was built before his father gave him a deed of the land on which it stood, on the 8th of April, 1702. It stood on the east side of High street, in front of the present site of John Riley's house. On his death it was distributed equally among his brother and sisters, from whom, by numerous conveyances, it passed into the hands of Matthew Clark, their only surviving brother. Here he died, September 24, 1751, and, partly by deed and partly by will, the house became the property and home of Matthew Clark, Jr. He died without children November 1, 1792, and devised the house to Matthew Clark, son of his nephew, Dan. Clark. This Matthew, the great-great-grandson of the first John Clark, lived in New Britain, and having no use for the house sold it October 8, 1794, to Romanta Norton, who sold it February 14, 1798, to Shubael Porter. The latter dying February 10, 1825, devised it to his son Erastus, who died August 8, 1846, giving it in his will to his two sisters, Sukey, wife of Samuel Dickinson, and Anna, wife of John Sweet. The latter and their heirs conveyed it in 1871 to John Riley, who, after using it as a barn for a few years, pulled it down in the summer of 1880.

Sergeant John Clark died intestate, and since no children are mentioned in the distribution of his estate, if he ever had any they must have died young. The order for the distribution of his estate was issued April 9, 1712, and is here given in proof of the relationship of the parties therein named. The distribution itself is recorded at great length in the town records of Farmington.

" Upon the motion and request of Samuel Woodruff Sen'—of Farmington who married with Rebecca Clark one of the sisters of Serg' John Clark late of said Farmington deceased praying that this Court would make out an order for the distribution and division of the lands and real estate of the said John Clark deceased to and among the bretheren and sisters of the said deceased or their survivors respectively according to law, which lands and real estate as by the inventory thereof appears to amount to the sum of 162£, 0s., 0d. This Court do therefore order that the said lands and real estate of the said John Clark deceased shall be distributed and divided as follows viz:—To Matthew Clark brother of the deceased the sum or value of 16£, 4s., 0d. To the heirs of Elizabeth Gridley deceased late wife to Thomas Gridley Sen. of said Farmington and sister to the said John Clark deceased the sum or value of 16£, 4s., 0d. To Rebecca Woodruff wife to the aforesaid Samuel Woodruff the sum of

16£, 4s., 0d. To Mary Huntington, wife to Samuel Huntington of Lebanon the sum of 16£, 4s., 0d. To Sarah Root
the wife of Thomas Root of aforesaid Lebanon the sum of
16£, 4s., 0d.

To Martha Clark wife of Thomas Clark of Milford the
sum or value of 16£, 4s. 0d.

To Abigail Pixley wife to Joseph Pixley of Westfield the sum
of £16, 4s., 0d. To the heirs of Hannah Woodruff deceased
late wife of Joseph Woodruff of said Farmington the sum of
£16, 4s., 0d. To Rachel Jones, Widow Relict of Caleb Jones
late of Hebron deceased the sum of 16£, 4s., 0d. To Mercy
Clark of Milford sister to the said John Clark deceased the
sum of 16£, 4s., 0d. And this Court do order and appoint
Mr. John Wadsworth, Mr. Daniel Andrews and Mr. Thomas
Stanley Senr of said Farmington or any two of them to dis-
tribute and divide the said estate accordingly and make
report and return thereof to this Court on or before the first
Monday of May next ensuing at which Court the said Matthew Clark administrator on that estate is ordered to appear
and render account of his administration thereon in order to
have his *Quietus Est* granted."

3.

Matthew[3] (*John*[1]) born before 1674; m. about 1704 Ruth,
daughter of John and Mary (Howkins) Judd. He died September 24, 1751, and left an estate which was inventoried at
£3,966, 15s., 6d, including 310 acres of land. His will is
recorded as follows:

"In the name of God, Amen. The 11th day of September
in the year of our Lord 1751, I, Matthew Clark Senr of
Farmington in the county of Hartford and colony of Con
necticut, in New England being well stricken in years and

weak in body but of perfect mind and memory, thanks be to
God therefor, calling to mind the mortality of my body and
knowing that 'tis appointed unto men once to die do ordain
this my last will and testament, that is to say first and prin-
cipally of all I give and recommend my soul in to the hands
of God that made it, hoping through the death and passion
of my Saviour Jesus Christ to have full and free pardon of
all my sins and to inherit Eternal Life, and my body I commit it to the earth to be decently buried nothing doubting but
at the General Resurection of the Just I shall receive the
same again by the almighty power of God, and as to such
worldly estate as God has blessed [me] with in this life, I
give and dispose of the same in the following manner and
form.—First I will that all those debts and duties as I do owe
in right or conscience to any manner of person or persons
shall be well and truly paid in convenient time after my
decease. Imprimis unto my well beloved Ruth Clark I give
and bequeath one third part of my Real Estate or estate of
Housing & lands to be used and improved by her, and she is
to have the profits and effects thereof during her natural life
and one third part of my moveable estate to be at her own
dispose forever. Item unto my two sons viz:—John and
Matthew Clark I give and bequeath to them and their heirs
and assigns forever all my lands both meadow & upland both
divided and undivided in equal proportion between them both
for quantity and quality, also all my housing and barns and
also all my moveable estate of what kind or sort forever, that
I shall stand possessed of at my death and not legally conveyed away in my life time, they or their heirs paying to my
daughters viz. Mary and Ruth the sums hereafter in this my
will given to them. Item unto my two daughters viz. Mary
Smith & Ruth Woodruff I give and bequeath besides what I

have formerly given them, I give to each of them the sum of one hundred pounds in bills of public credit of the old tenor to be paid to them by my aforenamed two sons John and Matthew Clark in convenient time after my decease and further I do ordain and appoint my two sons John and Matthew Clark to be executors to this my last will and testament. In witness whereof I the said Matthew Clark Sen.ʳ have hereunto set my hand and seal the day and year above written. Signed, Sealed, Published and Declared by the said Matthew Clark to be his last will and testament in presence of us witnesses.

MATTHEW CLARK [A SEAL.]

JOSEPH HOOKER.
MATTHEW JUDD.
SETH NORTON.

His children were :

    i. RUTH, b. Dec. 16, 1706 ; d. Jan. 3, 1706–7.
    ii. MATTHEW, b. May 8, 1708 ; d. Dec. 12, 1716.
12. iii. MARY, b. April 14, 1710 ; baptized April 15, 1710.
13. iv. JOHN, b. Sept. 1, 1712.
14. v. RUTH, b. May 14, 1716.
15. vi. MATTHEW, b. Dec. 19, 1719.

4. GRIDLEY.

Elizabeth² (*John¹*) married Dec. 25, 1679, Thomas Gridley, son of Thomas and Mary (Seymour) Gridley, and died April, 1696. Thomas Gridley, Jr., was born in Hartford, "the first week in August, 1650." After the death of his father, which occurred sometime before June 12, 1655, his mother married John Langdon the administrator on the estate, and removed to Farmington with her children, Samuel, Thomas, and Mary. By an order of the court, " John Lanckton is admitted Administrator to ye whole estate and is to pay all

Debts, well educate ye children, learning ye sonnes to read
and write and ye daughter to read and sow well." Thomas
Gridley was one of the Eighty-four Proprietors of Farmington. His house stood on the east side of Main Street, about
half a mile south of the church, a little north of a lane which
runs eastwardly at right angles to Main Street. The land
on which it stood is a part of the grounds belonging to the
house of Allan D. Vorce. He died in 1712 (*Historical Dis-
course by Noah Porter*, 1840, p. 60,) or in 1742, if Bronson is
correct. (*See History of Waterbury*, p. 26.)

Their children were:

i. INFANT, born and died June, 1681.
ii. INFANT, born and died Sept., 1682.
iii. THOMAS, b. June, 1683 : baptized June 17, 1683, m.
     Aug. 3, 1710, Elizabeth Brownson, born April 4, 1688,
     and died between July 27, and Aug. 10, 1767, daugh-
     ter of Samuel and Sarah (Gibbs) Brownson; Thomas
     died Jan. 22, 1754, and was known as Thomas of Ken-
     sington.
iv. JOHN, b. Oct., 1684; baptized Oct. 5, 1684; m. May 30,
     1711, Elizabeth Ellsworth of Windsor, *probably* born
     Jan. 22, 1683, daughter of Josiah, Jr., and Martha
     (Taylor) Ellsworth. (*See Stiles' History of Windsor*,
     p. 599.) John d. May 13, 1769, being then a resident
     of Simsbury. Elizabeth died June 16, 1756.
v. SAMUEL, b. March 1685–6; baptized March 21, 1685–6;
     m. Aug. 21, 1723, Abigail Hough, who died Jan. 3,
     1724–5. (He m. 2d. Dec. 12, 1727, Rebecca Cham-
     berlin of Lebanon, Ct., who died aged 83 years. He
     d. in 1772. *See letter of W. S. Gridley.*)
vi. MARY, b. Jan., 1687–8; baptized Feb. 5, 1687–8; m.
     Dec. 23, 1709, William Judd, baptized July 3, 1687,
     son of Philip and Hannah (Loomis) Judd. He re-
     moved to Waterbury and thence to Danbury.

vii.   JONATHAN, b. Oct., 1690; baptized Nov. 2, 1690; m.
       Nov. 17, 1714, Mary Pinney of Windsor, (*perhaps*
       Mary, daughter of Isaac and Sarah (Clark) Pinney,
       born March 4, 1690. *See Stiles' Windsor*, 746, *and
       Goodwin's Genealogical Notes*, 39.) He died Nov. 16,
       1778.

viii. ELIZABETH, b. Oct., 1693; baptized Oct. 29, 1693; m.
       Dec. 6, 1711, Benjamin Andrews, son of Benjamin and
       Mary (Smith) Andrews. (He was born Aug. 20,
       1683, and died Jan. 24, 1728, and is said to have been
       the first person buried in the Oak Hill Cemetery in
       Southington, Ct. *Andrews Memorial*, 62 and 72.)

ix.   " LAST CHILD," b. March, 1695–6; d. March, 1695–6.

5.   WOODRUFF.

Rebecca[2] (*John*[1]) m. 1686, as the date is given by Savage,
Samuel Woodruff, born Aug. 26, 1661, son of Matthew and
Hannah Woodruff of Farmington. He is said to have been
the first settler of Southington, Ct., whither he removed with
his family about the year 1698. He was a man of unusual
size, a noted hunter and trapper, and lived on very friendly
terms with the Indians. He died Jan. 28, 1742, aged 83,
and his wife Aug. 4, 1737, aged 65, if their gravestones,
standing side by side in Southington, can be trusted. If the
date of his birth on the   ords is correct, he must have
been 81 years 5 mon   owing for old style, and she
must have had her   the age of 14. The figures on
the stones are pl

Their child'

i.   SAMUE   0, 1686–7; m. July 10, 1718, Esther
      Bir   o. 28, 1696–7 in Farmington, and died
      J   , daughter of Samuel and Esther (Wood-
                  .. Samuel Woodruff d. Feb., 1766.

ii.   JON   Nov. 30, 1688; m. July 10, 1711, Sarah
      Langdon,   il 29, 1685, daughter of Joseph and

4

Susannah (Root) Langdon. Sarah outlived her husband. She resigned the office of administratrix Sept. 6, 1715. He d. April 29, 1712.

iii. REBECCA, b. Feb. 4, 1690 ; m. Nov. 18, 1714, William Smith, born Jan. 8, 1687-8, died July 26, 1718, son of Samuel and Ruth (Porter) Smith. She outlived him and m. 2d, James Pike who died Jan. 31, 1762. By Southington Church Records " Old Mrs. Pike died October 20, 1759." There is very little doubt that this was Rebecca. She was living April 10, 1759, when James Pike executed his will.

iv. RUTH, b. Feb. 15, 1692 ; m. Jan. 1, 1712-13, Nathaniel Porter, born March 28, 1692, son of Thomas and Abigail (Cowles) Porter. She d. Nov. 14, 1713, when Nathaniel married June 1, 1715, Joanna Smith, born Oct. 15, 1692, daughter of Joseph and Lydia Smith.

v. EBENEZER, b. Dec. 27, 1694 ; m. 1st (in 1728, *see Timlow's Southington*, cclx) Sarah (Gridley) Cowles, widow, daughter of Samuel and Mary (Humphreys) Gridley. She was baptized July 8, 1694 ; m. March 15, 1721-2, Nathaniel Cowles, born April 28, 1698 (died in 1725, *according to Wm. S. Porter*), son of Nathaniel and Phebe (Woodruff) Cowles. She died Feb. 5, 1743-4, when Ebenezer m. 2d, Sept. 27, 1744, · Esther ———, and d. between April 15 and May 20, 1747.

vi. DANIEL, b. Nov. 2, 1696 : m. Oct. 15, 1719, Lydia Smith, born Nov. 20, 1697, died Aug. 31, 1785, aged 88, daughter of Ephraim and Rachel (Cole) Smith. Daniel d. April 12, 1785, aged 89.

vii. DAVID, b. Feb. 27, 1698-9. Said to have been the first white child born in Southington ; m. Jan. 18, 1721-2, Mary Porter, born September, 1700, d. May 14, 1784, aged 83, daughter of Samuel and Martha (Freeman) Porter. David d. Jan. 14, 1767, aged 68, according to gravestone, or Jan. 13, according to church record.

viii. HEZEKIAH, b. Aug. 9, 1701 ; m. Dec. 3, 1730, Sarah

McKune of Stratford, b. Nov. 5, 1704, died July 20,
1785, aged 80, daughter of Robert and Sarah (Wil-
coxson) McKune. Hezekiah d. March 5, 1791, aged
89.

ix. RACHEL, b. Nov. 20, 1703; m. Dec. 7, 1727, John Bell;
d. Oct. 20, 1768. He married 2d, Lydia (Collins of
Kensington, Jan. 16, 1771, who died April 23, 1777,
in her 65th year. *Timlow's Southington*, page xxvi).
He died Oct. 27, 1776, aged 74 (*gravestone*).

x. ABIGAIL, b. Feb. 26, 1705; d. Nov. 8, 1707.

xi. JOHN, b. April 5, 1708; m. Aug. 11, 1729, Eunice
Wiard, born Jan. 15, 1712, daughter of John, Jr., and
Phebe (Hurlbut) Wiard. She died May 7, 1761, and
he m. 2d, Abigail (Ives. See *Timlow's Southington*,
cclxi.) She died Feb. 26, 1805, aged 92. John d.
Oct. 17, 1794.

xii. (REDE, b. 1710; d. Aug. 4, 1753. See *Timlow's Southington*, cclviii.)

6. HUNTINGTON.

Mary[2] (*John*[1]) b. about 1667. By the distribution of the
estate of Sergeant John[2] Clark on the 9th of April, 1712, it
appears that his sister Mary was the wife of "Samuel Huntington of Lebanon." Now the only Samuel Huntington of a
suitable age in Lebanon at this time seems to have been
Lieut. Samuel, who, moreover, is said in the Huntington
Memoir, page 74, to have been born in Norwich, March 1,
1665, and to have married a Mary Clark, Oct. 29, 1686.
Sarah, a sister of Mary[2] Clark, married Thomas Root and
moved to Lebanon about the same time with Samuel Hunt
ington. These two men were among the fifty-one original
proprietors of Lebanon, as appears in Hoadley's edition of
Conn. Colonial Records,. iv, 514. The following extract is
from the Huntington Memoir: "He removed to Lebanon in
1700, having sold his house-lot and house in Norwich for a

parsonage. Before his removal he had become a public man, having filled several offices, being as early as 1692 appointed constable, having already been one of the Townsmen. How well he was thought of in Norwich appears from his appointment by the citizens of Norwich, ten years after his removal to Lebanon, on a committee to locate the new meeting-house, about which a serious dispute had arisen. The site chosen by the committee was not approved by the town, and the church was erected upon another spot. But a few years vindicated the wisdom of the committee, as was abundantly testified by a second church built upon the place selected by them.

"He was a large land-owner both in Norwich and Lebanon, and for his services as a military manager, was entered on the records as Lieutenant, a title in those days won only by a true martial bearing and intended as a most honorable distinction.

"His wife's name appears on the list of the Lebanon church in 1701, but his own was not added until 1707.

"He died in Lebanon, May 10, 1717, and his wife, Oct. 5, 1743."

The two last named dates are given as above in *Morgan's Early Lebanon*, 159, but in the *N. E. Historical and Genealogical Register*, xii, 56, we have the following copies of epitaphs in the ancient graveyard at Lebanon, Conn. :

> Here lyes ye Body of
> Lieut Samuel Huntington
> Gentleman who died
> May ye 19 1717 in y^e
> 52 year of his age.

> In memory of Mrs.
> Mary Huntington the wife
> of Lieutenant Samuel Huntington
> who died Oct. 5, 1743
> in the 77th year of her age.

Lieut. Samuel was son of Deacon Simon and Sarah (Clark) Huntington.

His children were:

i. ELIZABETH, b. in Norwich, April 24, 1689: m. Feb. 23, 1710, Moses Clark of Lebanon, born 1683, died Sept. 18, 1749, son of Daniel and Hannah (Pratt) Clark. She d. Dec. 27, 1761.

ii. SAMUEL, b. in Norwich, Aug. 28, 1691; m. in Lebanon, Dec. 4, 1722, Hannah Metcalf, born Jan. 17, 1702, died Oct. 14, 1791, daughter of Jonathan and Hannah (Avery) Metcalf. He d. in his 94th year.

iii. CALEB, b. in Norwich, Feb. 8, 1693-4; m. Jan. 28, 1720, Lydia Griswold, born May 28, 1696, daughter of Capt. Samuel and Susannah (Huntington) Griswold.

iv. MARY, b. in Norwich, Oct. 1, 1696: d. in Lebanon, July 30, 1712.

v. REBECCA, b. in Norwich, February. 1698-9; m. June 20, 1717, Joseph Clark of Lebanon, born Dec. 31, 1691, died Sept. 10, 1769, aged 77, son of Capt. William and Hannah (Strong) Clark.

vi. SARAH, b. in Lebanon Oct. 22, 1701.

vii. JOHN, b. in Lebanon May 17, 1706; m. in Lebanon Mehitable Metcalf, born July 26, 1706, daughter of Jonathan and Hannah (Avery) Metcalf and sister of his brother Samuel's wife.

viii. SIMON, b. in Lebanon Aug. 15, 1708; m. May 15, 1735, Sarah Huntington, born April 28, 1718, died Nov. 7, 1791, daughter of Deacon Ebenezer and Sarah (Leffingwell) Huntington. Simon d. in Lebanon Aug. 22, 1753.

This account of the children of Mary[2] Clark is mostly from the *Huntington Family Memoir*, with slight additions from *Goodwin's Genealogical Notes*, the *Strong Genealogy*, 1472, and *Morgan's Early Lebanon*.

7.   ROOT.

Sarah² (*John*¹) b.   , m. Thomas Root, born April
13, 1667, in Northampton, died 1726, in Lebanon, Conn., son
of Joseph and Hannah (Haynes) Root. Their children
were :

i. SARAH, b. 1692, in Northampton.
ii. MARTHA, b. Oct. 12, 1693, in Northampton; d. young.
iii. THOMAS, b. Sept. 13, 1796, in Northampton; d. young.
iv. HANNAH, b. May 12, 1699, in Lebanon; m. Nov. 6,
1718, Benoni Clark, born Feb. 1, 1693–4, son of
Capt. William and Hannah (Strong) Clark.
v. MARY, b. Feb. 14, 1701, in Lebanon.
vi. THOMAS, b. Dec. 13, 1705, in Lebanon; m. 1st, ———;
m. 2d, Dec. 28, 1732, Hannah (Rose) Norton, widow
of Thomas Norton. Thomas Norton was born 1660,
married Hannah Rose June 7, 1700, and died May 2,
1729. The last five dates are from Farmington Church
and Town Records, from which last source we learn
that Sarah, the youngest child of Thomas and Hannah
Root, was born June 5, 1733, at which date Hannah
must have been at least fifty years old. Still I know
of no other Hannah, widow of Thomas Norton, for
Thomas Root to have married. "Widow Hannah
Root," probably the same, died Jan. 23, 1762.
vii. ELEAZER, b. 1706 in Lebanon ; d. Aug. 11, 1706.
viii. MARTHA, b. Feb. 11, 1708.
ix. EXPERIENCE, b. Feb. 10, 1711 or Jan. 10, according to
Morgan's Early Lebanon.

This account of Sarah² Clark and her children is compiled
from the *Root Genealogical Record*, 108 and 115, and *Dwight's
Strong Genealogy*, 1473, except as otherwise indicated.

8.

Martha² (*John*¹) m. Nov. 22, 1703, Deacon Thomas Clark,
widower, of Milford, Conn., born Jan. 22, 1668, and died

Feb. 12, 1727–8, aged 60, son of Thomas and Hannah (Gilbert) Clark. Their children were:

i. REBECCA, b. Oct. 4, 1704; baptized Oct. 8, 1704; m. March 4, 1730–1 Phineas Camp of Milford, known as Sergeant Phineas, who died probably in 1761. Administration was granted to his widow Rebecca, March 2, 1761.

ii. MARTHA, b. Jan. 15, 1705–6; baptized Jan. 20, 1705–6; m. before Feb. 11, 1727–8 Jonathan Treat, born March 17, 1701, and died May 31, 1779, aged 78, son of Robert and Abigail (Camp) Treat. Martha died Jan. 12, 1775, aged 46. The following extract is from *Farmington Town Records*, iv, 535. "Whereas we Jonathan Treat and his wife Martha formerly Martha Clark and Rebeckah Clark all of the town of Milford in the county of New Haven in the colony of Connecticut in New England have right unto two acres of land contained in a grant of land made by the town of Farmington in their meeting January 10th 1695–6 unto our uncle Sergt. John Clark," March 12, 1728–9.

iii. ANN, b. Oct. 9, 1707; baptized Oct. 12, 1707; d. May 29, 1708.

iv. THOMAS, b. March 22, 1708–9; baptized March 27, 1709. Was living as late as May 7, 1733, when his brother Jared chose him as guardian.

v. ABIGAIL, baptized June 10, 1711. Was not named in her father's will Feb. 11, 1727–8, and therefore probably died young.

vi. KEZIAH, baptized Nov. 23, 1712; (*probably* m. March 25, 1731, John Buckingham, born Aug. 14, 1707, son of Gideon and Sarah (Hunt) Buckingham. See *Chapman's Buckingham Family*, 20.)

vii. JONATHAN, b. March, 1717; baptized March 3, 1716–7; d. April 9, 1717.

viii. JARED, b. Jan. 28, 1718–9; m. Martha ———; d. 1789. His will was dated May 18, 1789, and presented in court June 3, 1789. Her dower was set out to the widow Martha Dec. 7, 1789.

9.   PIXLEY.

Abigail[2] (*John*[1]) m. Aug. 23, 1699, Joseph Pixley, born at Northampton, Mass., March 9, 1676, son of William and Sarah (Lawrence) Pixley. He removed to Westfield, Mass , and thence about 1730 to Great Barrington. Their children were:

i.   JONAH, b. March 3, 1701 ; m. 1725, Elizabeth Hanum; published his intention of marriage Oct. 16, 1725.

ii. JOSEPH, b. March 4, 1703 ; published his intention of marriage to Sarah Smith Dec. 11, 1730.

iii. ABIGAIL, b. May 29, 1705. *Probably* m. Dec. 1728. Isaac Fowler, born Nov. 12, 1697, died at Westfield May 20, 1790, aged 92, son of John and Mercy (Miller) Fowler. Abigail Fowler died at Westfield June 28, 1759.

iv. MOSES, b. June 9, 1707 : m. Sarah Lyon; published his intention of marriage to her Sept. 6, 1730; d. 1771.

v.   JOHN, b. Oct. 22, 1709; published his intention of marriage to Mary Hall Oct. 23, 1736.

vi. JONATHAN, b. Jan. 17, 1711: d. June 17, 1775.

vii. DAVID, b. March 21, 1714 ; (m. 1st, a sister of Jacob Cooper of West Springfield; m. 2d, Abigail (King) Bliss, widow of Dr. Peletiah Bliss, Jr., who was born March 23, 1723, married Oct. 2, 1746, and died Dec. 26, 1756. See *Stockbridge, Past and Present, by Miss Jones*, 150, and *Bliss Genealogy*, 74 and 650.)

viii. CLARK, b. Oct. 3, 1724.

10.   WOODRUFF.

Hannah[2] (*John*[1]), baptized April 4, 1680; "born a few days before;" m. Sergt. Joseph Woodruff, born 1679 in Farmington, and called thirteen years old in the inventory of the estate of his father, John Woodruff, made May 16, 1692. Joseph

married 2d, April 15, 1708, Elizabeth Curtiss born November
13, 1681, daughter of John and Lydia Curtiss of Wethersfield. His will was dated January 16, 1729–30, and the
inventory of his estate was made March 24, 1731–2, his
widow Elizabeth outliving him. He left nine children. The
children by Hannah Clark were:

  i. HANNAH, b. Aug. 29, 1704; m. (Aug. 13, 1729, David
      Clark, born Sept. 5, 1705, in North Haven, son of
      Samuel and Mary (Brown) Clark. •He lived in
      Flanders district in Southington. See *Sketches of
      Southington, H. B. Timlow*, page li.)

 ii. JOSIAH, b. Aug. 18, 1706; m. Dec. 19, 1733, Sarah
      Woodford of Farmington, born June 4, 1714, daughter
      of Joseph and Lydia (Smith) Woodford.

11.   JONES.

Rachel[2] (*John'*), m. Caleb Jones, who is named in Bar-
ber's Historical Collections of Connecticut as one of the ten
who commenced the settlement of Hebron in 1704. He was
probably son of Samuel and Mary (Bushnell) Jones. Caleb
died before January 16, 1711–2, when an inventory was made
of his estate, including "land at Saybrook, 33 acres at Oyster
River Quarter." Administration was granted April 7, 1712,
to his widow Rachel, who married January 26, 1713–4, Israel
Phelps of Enfield, Ct., whose wife Mary had died April 7,
1713. She was *probably* the Mary born at Salem, March 11,
1681, daughter of Robert and Abigail (Randall) Pease, who
is said in the Pease Genealogy to have married Israel Phelps
in 1703. Israel Phelps was appointed July 5, 1714, guardian
of his wife's children, Caleb Jones aged about 8 years, Sylvanus about 6, Mary about 5, and Hezekiah about 3. The
children of Rachel were:

  i. CALEB, b. about 1706; m. Nov. 10, 1730, Miriam Par-
 5

sons, born April 9, 1710, daughter of Samuel and
Hannah (Hitchcock) Parsons of Enfield.

ii.   SYLVANUS, b. about 1708.

iii. MARY, b. about 1709.

iv.   HEZEKIAH, b. about 1711.

Her children by Israel Phelps were:

v.   JOHN, b. Dec. 3, 1714; d. Oct. 27, 1722.

vi.   DAVID, b. Aug. 25, 1716: m. March 29, 1737, Mar-
      garet Colton, who died Feb. 16, 1810, aged 96, daugh-
      ter of Josiah and Margaret (Pease) Colton. David
      died Jan. 31, 1803, aged 86.

vii. JOHN, b. July, 1723.

viii. NOAH, b. March 16, 1726.

ix.   HANNAH, b. Nov. 19, 1731.

12.   SMITH.

Mary[3] (*Matthew*[2], *John*[1]), b. April 14, 1710; m. Nov. 1,
1733, Stephen Smith, born April 3, 1707, son of Samuel
Smith, *weaver*, and Ruth (Porter) Smith. They removed to
Southington. Their children were:

i.   RUTH, b. Sept. 13, 1734; d. Sept. 28, 1749.

ii.   SIBYL, b. May 5, 1737.

iii. MATTHEW, b. Jan. 1, 1739–40.

iv.   ITHAMAR, b. Nov. 22, 1742 (*Farmington Town Records*,
      vol. 7).

v.   HEMAN, baptized Jan. 9, 1742–3 (*Southington Church
      Records*): d. Oct. 2, 1749. Either the record of the
      birth of Ithamar or the baptism of Heman is wrong.
      The copy is correctly made.

vi.   MARY, baptized Feb. 29, 1745; d. Sept. 28, 1749.

vii. REBECCA, b. April 18, 1748.

viii. RUTH, b. April 29, 1750.

ix.   HEMAN 2d, b. Nov. 29, 1753. The following extract is
      from *Annals of Winchester, by John Boyd*, 178.
      " Heman Smith, from Goshen, this year [1788]
      bought and moved on to the farm of Noah Gleason on

the south part of Blue Street, which he occupied until
1801, when he sold out to Isaac Brownson, and removed to Vernon, N. Y. He was a man highly
esteemed, prominent in town affairs, and three times
a representative of the town between 1795 and 1800.
He was a son of Stephen Smith from Farmington, was
born in Goshen and married Hannah Dunning. He
left no record of his family in Winchester." The
will of Matthew³ Clark dated Aug. 2, 1790, names
"my nephew Heman Smith of Winchester." The
above-named nine children were all baptized in Southington, except the first, fourth, and ninth, of whose
baptism I find no record.

13.

John³ (*Matthew², John¹*), b. Sept. 1, 1712 ; m. Sept. 2,
1742, Elizabeth Newell, born Jan. 29, 1720–1, died Feb. 2,
1791, aged 70, daughter of Capt. John and Elizabeth (Haw-
ley) Newell. They lived on the Stanley Quarter road leading
from Farmington to New Britain, where Omri North lived
many years and his son Lucius J. North after him, until
1879. The old Clark house was moved back and is now used
as a barn. Although living within the territorial limits of
Great Swamp (Kensington) parish, Mr. Clark with the families of Daniel Hart and Thomas Stanley 2d, attended the
public worship of the old church of Farmington. After the
death of her husband, on the 10th of June, 1782, Elizabeth attended the New Britain church, and being partially deaf was
allowed to stand in the pulpit. Her remains are interred beside those of her husband in the Old Cemetery of Farmington.

Their children were :

16.   i. MERCY, b. Nov. 9, 1743.

      ii. MARY, b. Feb. 23, 1745 ; d. (Feb. 1814. Was a

school teacher, and kept school in New Britain in the
old Thomas Hooker house on the west side of East
Street, on the site of Amzi Judd's. She was never
married. *Andrews' New Britain*. 222.)

17. iii. MERVIN, b. Nov. 26, 1746.
18. iv. DAN, b. Aug. 11. 1748.
19. v. ABEL, b. 1750.
20. vi. RUTH, b. March 19, 1752.
21. vii. JOHN, b. March 18, 1754.
22. viii. HULDAH, b. 1756.
23. ix. ELIZABETH, b. May 14, 1758. (*Andrews' New Britain*, 194.)
    x. JANE, b. Nov. 20, 1763; m. Dec. 21, 1785, Elijah
Francis, born Jan. 6, 1760, died Oct. 30, 1846, aged
87, son of Elijah and Hannah (Buck) Francis. He
was a shoemaker and tanner, learning his trade of
Deacon Timothy Stanley. At the age of sixteen he
served in the Revolutionary Army as a teamster. He
lived in New Britain, in the valley east of Osgood
Hill, was a deacon in the church, and represented the
town of Berlin in the legislature several times. (*See
Andrews' New Britain*, 262.) Jane died Feb. 16,
1849, aged 85, and is buried with her husband, in New
Britain Cemetery.

14. WOODRUFF.

Ruth (*Matthew², John¹*), b. May 14, 1716; m. probably,
Robert Woodruff, born Oct. 8, 1710, son of Samuel and Mary
(Judd) Woodruff. I can find no record of this marriage.
Nevertheless Matthew² Clark names his daughter Ruth Woodruff in his will, Sept. 11, 1751. Also Robert names his wife
Ruth in his will, dated Nov. 8, 1781, which will was wit-
nessed by Matthew Clark, and there are numerous minor
reasons for believing it was this Woodruff who was the husband of Ruth. Robert Woodruff's house was in New Britain,

near the Wethersfield (now Newington) town line, his farm
being bounded north and west by highways. He died between
Nov. 8, 1781, and May 3, 1782, his wife outliving him. Robert
Woodruff was a prominent man in the parish of New Britain,
serving, as the records show, on numerous committees where
men of ability and sound judgment were needed. " To order
the affairs of the school in this society." " To procure our
rights of the loan-money that is lodged in the First Society
of Farmington, and the Society of Kensington." In the re-
peated attempts to settle a minister he was appointed at sun-
dry times " to apply to Mr. John Bunnell, ... to remove
the objections that lay in the way of his settling in the work
of the ministry amongst us." " To apply to the South Asso-
ciation of Hartford County, for their advice for some suitable
and orthodox candidate," etc. " To persuade said Associa-
tion to advise Mr. Fowler to preach in the society as a proba-
tioner." " To present the votes of this society to Mr. Amos
Fowler, and use his influence with him to tarry among us."
In the May Session of the legislature, in 1756, he was con-
firmed as " Ensign of the 13th company or trainband in the
6th Regiment in this Colony," but was usually known as Sergeant Robert Woodruff.

Their children were:

i.   SETH, b. 1744 ; d. Nov. 30, 1823, aged 79.
ii. AMOS, b. 1745 ; m. (Oct. 27, 1768, Sarah Clark, daugh-
     ter of Joseph and Sarah (Curtiss) Clark. *See An-
     drews' History of New Britain*, 139) who died April
     20, 1824, aged 74. Amos died Feb. 1, 1828, aged 83.
iii. SARAH, b. Oct. 6, 1749 ; m. Dec. 31, 1777, William
     Walker of Rehoboth, Mass., born June 22, 1751, o. s.,
     and died Oct. 31, 1831, son of Caleb and Elizabeth
     (Perrin) Walker. Sarah died Sept. 1, 1789, when he
     married 2d, March 24, 1790, Mrs. Mary (Hutchinson)

Parmalee of Goshen, Ct. For this account of Sarah,
see *Walker Genealogy by J. B. R. Walker*, where may
be found a portrait and extended biographical sketch
of William Walker.

iv. RUTH, b. April 10, 1751; m. Elizur Whaples of Newington, Conn.. born 1755, baptized Dec 28, 1755, son of
Jonathan and Margaret (Woodruff) Whaples. Ruth
d. May 27, 1794. See *Andrews' History of New
Britain*.

15.

Matthew[3] (*Matthew*,[2] *John*[1]), b. Dec 19, 1719; m. May 8,
1746, Sarah Merrill, born 1719, ba,tized May 24, 1719, died
Nov. 16, 1785, aged 67, daughter of Lieut. Isaac and Sarah
(Cooke) Merrill. He married 2d, the widow Lydia Seymour,
born July 22, 1729, daughter of Lieut. Jacob and Mary
(Sedgwick) Kellogg. She married Dec. 1, 1748, Capt. Timothy Seymour of West Hartford, who died in 1784. After
the death of Matthew Clark, she married 3d, in September,
1803, Capt. Archibald McNeil of Litchfield, who died Jan. 31,
1813, aged 76, son of Capt. Archibald and Sarah McNeil,
concerning whom see Sketches and Chronicles of the Town
of Litchfield, by P. K. Kilbourne, pp. 80 and 251. Lydia
joined the church in Litchfield in 1804, and died in that
town Nov. 6, 1810, aged 81. Matthew Clark died Nov. 1,
1792, aged 73, and is buried by the side of his first wife in
the Old Cemetery of Farmington. His will, dated Aug. 2,
1790, names his wife Lydia, nephews Mervin Clark and Dan
Clark, his friend James Merrill, Matthew, son of the above-
mentioned Dan Clark, and his nephew Heman Smith of
Winchester.

16.   WADSWORTH.

Mercy[1] (*John*,[3] *Matthew*,[2] *John*[1]), b. Nov. 9, 1743; m.
December, 1766, as the date is given in *Andrews' New Britain*,

193, to William Wadsworth of Farmington, born Feb. 16, 1742, and died March 20, 1816, son of Capt. William and Ruth (Hart) Wadsworth. She died July 9, 1814, aged 71. Their graves are in the Old Cemetery of Farmington. He lived on the west side of Farmington Main street, on the site of a house built and occupied by his son, Deacon Sidney Wadsworth, and sold after the death of the latter to Ira Hadsell, and by him to Levi Risley, whose son now owns it. William Wadsworth is described by one now living, who well remembers him, as a man of more than ordinary intellect, but extremely willful and passionate. Illustrative of the latter disposition, he relates Mr. Wadsworth's contest with a vicious horse who had the habit of pulling back and breaking his halter on every possible occasion. To cure him of this propensity, or kill him, he cared little which, he led him down to a lot in the South Meadow, now owned by Henry W. Barbour, and tied him to a tree close to the steep river-bank, below which the river ran unusually deep. The vicious brute pulling back broke his halter, as was expected, and going heels over head into the river floundered about for a while, but finally swam ashore, a thoroughly cured and repentant animal. The children of William and Mercy Wadsworth were:

    i. DECIUS, b. Jan. 2, 1768. Graduated at Yale College in 1785, and entered as a law student the office of Judge John Trumbull, author of McFingal. In 1792 he accepted the commission of Captain of Artillery and Engineers in the U. S. Army. In 1800 he resigned and established himself in a mercantile business in Montreal. At the commencement of the war of 1812 he entered the ordnance department of the U. S. Army with the rank of Colonel, but on the reduction and reorganization of the army at the close of the war

he left the service and returned to his native state.
He died in New Haven on the 8th of November, 1821.
He never married.   An interesting obituary notice of
him may be found in the *National Intelligencer* for
Dec. 8, 1821.

ii.   ROMEO, b. April 2, 1769, in Farmington: d. Oct. 9. 1850,
      in Hartford, Conn.   From a letter of his son, William
      Romeo Wadsworth of San Francisco, Cal., it appears
      that Romeo m. 1st. Nov. 16, 1801, in Bennington, Vt.,
      Eunice Nichols, born May 31, 1779, died Sept. 17,
      1809.   He m. 2d, Sept. 9, 1817, at New Brunswick,
      N. J., Ann Margaret Fleming, born Dec. 29, 1783,
      died August. 1860, daughter of Samuel and Mary
      Teresa (Parsons) Fleming.

iii. GEORGE, b. Oct. 9, 1782: m. Feb. 28, 1808, at Burling-
      ton. Vt., Laura Lyman, born Oct. 17. 1788, died Jan.
      2, 1853, at Plattsburg, daughter of Ebenezer and Anne
      Lyman. He died at Washington. D. C., Sept. 23,
      1823.   See *Lyman Genealogy*, 103, and a letter of his
      daughter, Mrs. Laura W. Halsey of Plattsburg, N. Y.

iv.   SIDNEY, b. Nov. 17, 1786: m. March, 1812, Clarissa
      Buck, born March 12, 1786, died June 6, 1862, daugh-
      ter of Capt. Isaac and Prudence (Deming) Buck.   He
      was a deacon in the First Congregational Church of
      Farmington, and died Aug. 25, 1845.

Other children died in infancy, but the records of their births
and deaths cannot be arranged with certainty.

17.

Mervin[1] (*John,*[3] *Matthew,*[2] *John*), b. Nov. 26, 1746; m.
Jan. 18, 1773, Sarah Woodruff. born June 3, 1748, died Jan.
5, 1813, aged 65, daughter of Abraham and Sarah (North)
Woodruff. He died Aug. 17, 1825.   His christian name is
spelled Mervin in all papers written by himself which have
come under my notice.   His townsmen universally spelled it
Marvin.   Early in life Mervin lived in the East Farms school

district of Farmington, in the little house recently known as
the Samuel Miller house, situated at the end of the lane which
runs past the house now owned by William Alfred and before
him by Ira Bowen. This latter house Mervin built for his
own residence, and it was occupied after him by his son
Abraham. He was one of the seventy signers to an agreement made Sept. 3, 1774, "to be in readiness and duly
equipped with arms and ammunition to proceed to Boston for
the relief of our distressed and besieged brethren there." He
was actively engaged in the war of the Revolution, but in
what capacity is not clearly known. He is said to have been
at Danbury, Conn., when that place was burned by Tryon in
April, 1777, and was at one time in the camp at Horse Plains.
Uniting with the church in Farmington in 1771, during the
ministry of Rev. Timothy Pitkin, he maintained through his
whole life a most exemplary christian character. Upright
and conscientious in his business relations, with a scrupulous-
ness rarely seen, he lived to a good old age, beloved by all
about him, transmitting to his posterity the memory of
numberless kind and loving acts which is to them a most
precious inheritance. In extreme old age he was under the
illusion that every day was Sunday, and so, spending all his
time in the devotional exercises most dear to him, his life
passed gently away. His children were:

    i. JEMIMA, b. Jan. 18, 1775 ; d. May 11, 1815, un-
       married.
24. ii. ORNAN, b. Nov. 20, 1777.
25. iii. ABRAHAM, b. Sept. 5, 1780.
    iv. SARAH, b. Dec. 22, 1785 ; d. July 4, 1850.
26. v. HULDAH, b. April 3, 1789.
  6

18.

Dan (*John,* *Matthew,* *John*), b. Aug. 11, 1748; m. (see *Andrews' New Britain,* 193) Jan. 24, 1771, Lucy Stanley. born about 1744, died June 26, 1794, aged 50, daughter of Thomas and Mary (Francis) Stanley. He married, 2d, Oct. 25, 1795, Abi Lewis, daughter of Phinehas and Sarah (Norton) Lewis. He died Dec. 9, 1827, and is buried by the side of his first wife in the Old Cemetery of Farmington. In his will, which was dated Jan. 4, 1820, and proved Dec. 31, 1827, he gives his estate to his wife Abi, his son Matthew, his grandson Dan Clark 2d, and his granddaughter Abi. He lived in New Britain, Conn., on Clark Hill.

In the Justice Records of Gov. Treadwell in the year 1780 and onward, Dan Clark appears as a tythingman and grandjuror. Numerous young people of both sexes, some of whom afterwards became very prominent and influential citizens of the town, were brought by him before his Honor, usually for "playing and talking in the time of public worship against the Peace and Laws of the State," or for "playing one or more Games at Cards against the Peace and Laws of the State," and one man of an honorable family because "he not having the fear of God before his eyes, did on the Lord's Day, that is on the 15th day of instant October neglect to attend Public worship." Fine three shillings and costs. Mr. Clark, though no doubt a terror to evil doers, was only in sympathy with the times. Certainly his zeal did not equal that of another officer, noticed in the same record, who brought fifteen young people of the first families of the place before the same magistrate because "they did convene together at the Dwelling House of Nehemiah Street and refused to disperse until after nine of the Clock at Night." Fine six shillings. Case appealed to the County Court.

Child by his first marriage :

27.   i.   MATTHEW, b. Oct. 2, 1773.

19.

Abel (*John,*[2] *Matthew,*[2] *John*[1]), b. 1750 ; m. Jan. 6, 1774, Abigail Judd, born June 5, 1752, died April 27, 1829, daughter of James and Hannah (Andrews) Judd. He lived in the house formerly occupied by his father in Stanley Quarter, New Britain. He was one of the seventy signers of an agreement made the 3d of September, 1774, "to be in readiness and duly equipped with arms and ammunition to proceed to Boston for the relief of our distressed and besieged brethren there," but from ill health he took no active part in the war of the Revolution, which soon followed. Abel died April 27, 1824, aged 74, and was interred in the old cemetery of New Britain, where the remains of his wife also rest. They died on the same day of the same month, if their epitaphs can be trusted. His will was dated April 27, 1814, and proved May 21, 1824, by which he gave his estate to his wife Abigail, his son John, his daughter Mary Andrews, and his grandchildren Elizur Clark, Cornelia Andrews, John Clark Andrews, Mary Andrews, and Ophelia Webster Clark.

Their children were :

       i.   SAMUEL, b. Oct. 30, 1774 ; d. Nov. 6, 1774, according to two separate entries in *Farmington Town Records*, vol. 17, pp. 431 and 445, but the gravestone reads Dec. 6, 1774, aged 6 days. Probably November is correct.

28. ii.   MANLY, b. April 1, 1776.

     iii.   ABIGAIL, b. 1780 : d. May 7, 1785, aged 5.— (*Gravestone.*)

29. iv.   MARY, b. Sept. 25, 1784 (*Andrews' Memorial*, 234).

30.   v.   JOHN, b. March 20, 1787 (*Andrews' New Britain*, 253).

31. vi. SYLVESTER, b. Feb. 18, 1789 (*Stephen Hart and his Descendants*, 505).

20.   STANLEY.

Ruth (*John,³ Matthew,² John¹*), b. March 19, 1752; m. Jan. 6, 1774, Seth Stanley, born March 18, 1751, died May 5, 1823, aged 72, at Stanley Corners, N. Y., son of Deacon Noah and Ruth (Norton) Stanley. He built the house in Stanley Quarter, New Britain, which burned down while owned by Martin Brown, in 1860. Here they lived until they removed in 1795 to Ontario Co., N. Y. She died Sept. 13, 1796, aged 44, and is buried in Canandaigua, N. Y. Children:

i. ASA, b. Nov. 21, 1774: m. Tirza Hayden; d. Oct. 24, 1851, at Akron, Ohio, where he was a merchant and farmer.

ii. CRUGER, b. Nov. 19, 1775; m. Sally Reed, born April 4, 1783: died April 14, 1858, daughter of John and Irene (Parish) Reed. Cruger d. May 3, 1815, at Canandaigua, N. Y., where he was a farmer.

iii. ERASTUS, b. Oct. 22, 1776: m. March 18, 1801, Temperance Smith, born Nov. 27, 1778, and died Feb. 25, 1847, in Phelps, N. Y., daughter of Henry and Catharine (Leonard) Smith. He lived at Canandaigua, N. Y., where he died Jan. 20, 1836.

iv. HORATIO, b. Nov. 24, 1777; d. at sea June 29, 1800. Buried in New Haven, Ct. Was unmarried.

v. SALINA, b. Oct. 10, 1779; m. 1st Sally Welch; m. 2d Lois Whitmore: m. 3d 1814 Rachel Smith, born 1792 at Gloucester, Essex Co., Mass., died 1877 at Geneva, N. Y., daughter of John and Betsey Williams. He d. Jan. 1, 1858, at Geneva, N. Y.

vi. NANCY, b. Jan. 2, 1781: m. John McCullough; d. Feb. 6, 1815.

vii. KATY, b. Jan. 15, 1782; d. March 7, 1811, at Canandaigua, N. Y. Was unmarried.

viii. JONATHAN, b. March 7, 1783; m. Sophronia Boughton; d. Aug. 8, 1817.

ix. SETH, b. June 6, 1781; m. April 17, 1807, Sally McKinney, born Nov. 7, 1789, died Dec. 18, 1819, daughter of Daniel McKinney. Seth d. July 3, 1837, according to the Stanley Bible, but 1834 according to a letter of Mrs. Mary Cornelia Stambach, of Hamburg, N. Y., daughter of Seth.

x. RUTH, b. Nov. 14, 1785; d. Aug. 27, 1806.

xi. CYRUS, b. April 8, 1787; d. April 24, 1787, aged 16 days (*Gravestone in New Britain*).

xii. HULDAH, b. March 26, 1788; m. Jan. 8, 1814, James Catlin, born Dec. 24, 1788, in Lennox, Mass., died May 4, 1872, son of John and Dinah (Look) Catlin. She d. in Rushville, N. Y., Feb. 10, 1866, aged 78, or 1868, according to her son, S. S. Catlin.

xiii. CALEB WALKER, b. Nov. 20, 1790; d. Nov. 23, 1793, aged 3 years and 3 days (*Gravestone in New Britain*).

xiv. DAUGHTER not named, b. and d. March 25, 1792 (*Gravestone in New Britain*).

xv. LUCIUS, b. April 5, 1793; m. May 1, 1817, Sally Runyan, born Sept. 27, 1797, and died March 9, 1837, daughter of Vincent and Elizabeth (Wolverton) Runyan. He m. 2d Sept. 13, 1838, Mrs. Polly Whedon, who was born March 14, 1795, married Dec. 8, 1813, Calvin Whedon, and is now living, daughter of John and Mary Gray. Lucius d. Jan. 5, 1871.

xvi. ELIZABETH, b. Nov. 18, 1794; m. John McKnight. Now living at Romulus, Seneca Co., N. Y.

My authority for this account of the sixteen children of Ruth' Clark is a "Copy from the Old Family Bible of the Stanleys, made by N. Curtis Stanley, Esq., of Logansport, Indiana," verified and supplemented by letters from Mrs. Ansel DeBow, daughter of Cruger (ii) of Canandaigua, N. Y.; Miss N. M. Stanley, daughter of Erastus (iii) of Phelps,

N. Y.; Mrs. Mary Cornelia Stambach, daughter of Seth (ix) of Hamburg, N. Y.; S. S. Catlin, Esq., son of Huldah (xii) of Rushville. N. Y.

21.

John[1] (*John,*[2] *Matthew,*[2] *John*[1]), b. March 18, 1754; m. April 9, 1794. Eunice Castle, removed to Canandaigua, N. Y.; d. 1819. His children:

    i.   John lived near Cleveland, Ohio; married and had two children. A persistent search fails to discover any further information of him.

32. ii. Eliza Jane, b. Dec. 5, 1797.

33. iii. Maria Green, b. Jan., 1802.

22.   WALKER.

Huldah[1] (*John,*[2] *Matthew,*[2] *John*[1]), b. 1756; m. Caleb Walker of Rehoboth, Mass., born April 5, 1753, died Aug. 10, 1790, son of Caleb and Elizabeth (Perrin) Walker. Caleb was a brother of William Walker, who married Sarah Woodruff (14, iii), first cousin of Huldah. He served in the war of the revolution under Col. Timothy Walker, died at Canandaigua, N. Y., and was buried in Lennox, Mass. They had one son.

    i.   Caleb Richard, b. Feb. 8, 1778; m. and had five children. (See *Walker Genealogy by J. B. R. Walker,* 174, 245, 305.)

23.   ANDREWS.

Elizabeth[1] (*John,* *Matthew,*[2] *John*[1]), b. May 14, 1758; m. 1779, Moses Andrews, born April 7, 1755, died July 20, 1848, son of Moses and Lydia (Root) Andrews. They lived on the road which leads from New Britain to Plainville, near the Quinnipiac River, about two miles west of New Britain Center. While this house was building they lived one year in the Demas Warner house, a few rods northwest of the new one on the hill still called Demas Hill. He was one of nine sons, seven of whom were in the war of the revolution. They removed about the year 1800 to Montague, Mass., where she died Dec. 8, 1840, aged 82. Their children, all born in New Britain, were:

i. SIDNEY, b. March 8, 1780: m. Oct. 24, 1804, Mary Clark (29), born Sept. 25, 1784, died Dec. 29, 1862, daughter of Abel and Abigail (Judd) Clark. Sidney d. Feb. 20, 1864.

ii. NOAH, b. March 19, 1782; m. Feb. 22, 1807, Ruth Griswold, born Aug. 23, 1790, died Oct. 28, 1856, daughter of Ezra and Ruth (Roberts) Griswold of Simsbury. He removed to Worthington, Ohio, and d. June 5, 1857, aged 75.

iii. BEULAH, b. April 6, 1784: m. Sept., 1801, at Suffield, Ct., Dr. J. H. Hills, and removed to Ohio, d. June 29, 1866, aged 82.

iv. BETSEY, b. June 22, 1786: went to Montague, Mass., with her father, m. at Columbus, Ohio, April 17, 1817, John Wallace. After his death she m. 2d, —— Handley. She d. Aug. 15, 1856.

v. CYNTHIA, b. Feb. 20, 1788; m. April 18, 1818, Eliphalet Bunker of Worthington, Ohio: m 2d, —— Pinney, and lived in Columbus, Ohio, d. Jan. 1, 1867.

vi. CATHARINE, b. June 8, 1790: m. Nov. 24, 1813, Romeo Francis, b. May 30, 1790, died March 30, 1849, son of James and Sylvia (Stanley) Francis of New Britain. He was in early life a school-master and farmer. She d. Feb. 26, 1867, in New York.

vii. JESSE, b. Oct. 28, 1792; m. Jan. 11, 1818, Sarah Alvord of Greenfield, Mass., born Jan. 27, 1796. He died Feb. 23, 1866.

viii. NANCY, b. Feb. 4, 1796; m. March 8, 1818, Thomas Russell of Deerfield, Mass.; m. 2d, Dec. 26, 1841, John Ortt of Greenfield, Mass.

This account of the children of Elizabeth⁴ Clark, is from the *Andrews' Memorial*, 135, 234, 235, and the manuscript Family Record of John Clark Andrews, son of (**29.**).

21.

Ornan⁵ (*Mervin¹, J.Ln³, Matthew², John¹*), b. Nov. 20, 1777, according to Farmington Town Records, or Nov. 23, as appears in a family bible; m. 1805, Lucy White, born July 22, 1784, died April 13, 1863, daughter of Joseph and Lucy (Bulkley) White. Ornan d. Feb. 14, 1815, and his widow married 2d, May 1, 1816, Jesse, son of Timothy and Lydia (Newell) Stanley, and was his second wife. Lydia above mentioned, was sister of Elizabeth, wife of John³ Clark (**13.**). About the time of his marriage, Ornan Clark built for himself a brick house in Farmington, on the "Old South Road" to Hartford, a few rods west of his father's house, on the same side of the road. This house was pulled down about thirty-five years ago, and its site is now covered by the flourishing apple orchard of William Alfred. Brick houses were then comparatively rare, and brick making an industry so little practiced in the vicinity, that Mr. Clark found it necessary to give his personal supervision and labors to the work, and over-exerting himself laid the foundation of the consumption of which he ultimately died. Opposite his house stood the building in which he carried on quite an extensive soap and candle business, in partnership with his brother Abraham, the product of their factory being shipped largely to the West Indies, until the war of 1812 put an end to the export business.

His children were:

34.   i.   HENRY WHITE, b. Feb. 23, 1807.
    ii. SARAH, b. July 18, 1809; m. Feb. 3, 1831, Oren Stanley North, born July 13, 1805, died Feb. 8, 1874,

son of Alvin and Anna (Stanley) North. They lived
in New Britain in the old Alvin North house, on the
east side of Stanley street, near East Main street, the
house having been moved there from the opposite side
of Stanley street. She is still living.

35. iii. MERVIN, baptized Jan., 1812.

25.

Abraham⁵ (*Mervin⁴, John³, Matthew², John¹*), b. Sept. 5,
1780; m. Feb. 13, 1809, Milicent Washburn, born July 23,
1784, in Middletown, Ct., and died March 9, 1863, in San
Francisco, Cal., daughter of Joseph and Ruth (Wetmore)
Washburn, and sister of Rev. Joseph Washburn, pastor of
the church in Farmington. He died in Chicago, Feb. 21,
1855. The following sketch is from the pen of Mrs. Jane
Eliza (Clark) Sanford (39), " Abram Clark was born Sept.
5, 1780, in Farmington, Ct. His childhood and youth were
spent in his birth place and here he received the education
usual at that time—that of the common school. At the age
of 29 he married Milicent Washburn, and for a time lived in
the house at the head of the lane near his father's. Later he
moved into the house with his father where he remained many
years. During the 'great revival' which occurred in connection with the labors of Dr. Nettleton, he joined the church
of which Dr. Noah Porter was pastor. His consistent, christian life through many vicissitudes attests the sincerity of his
profession. After his father's death, he bought of the other
heirs their interest in the house and farm, being ambitious to
keep the old homestead undivided. He was active and ener-
getic, and struggled on even after it became evident that, with
his growing family, he could not hold the place. In the fall
of 1830 he gave up and removed to New Haven, intending
to remain there while his eldest son went through Yale Col-

7

lege, and in order to give his younger children better oppor-
tunities for education. While residing here he learned that
a few families were about to unite for removal to the far
west (Illinois), and decided to join the party and seek a new
home. In this plan of removal, Dr. Leonard Bacon, with
whose church he was connected, manifested great interest,
and when the families, five in number, comprising twenty-
three persons, gathered at the house of Mr. Clark one day in
the fall of 1831, Dr. Bacon came to bid them good bye.
When the company were all ready to start, he proposed prayer,
and standing on the door steps surrounded by the several
families, and their friends assembled to take leave of them,
he offered prayer, committing them to the care of an ever-
present God, and with God's blessing, sent them on their way.

"The other families with whom Mr. Clark journeyed were
those of Deacon Chittenden, Mr. Bradley, Mrs. Wilson and
two sons, and a young couple named Plant. The party
reached Pittsburg on a dark and rainy evening after several
weeks of toilsome journeying over the Alleghanies. Here
the families having carriages took passage on board a steamer
bound down the Ohio and up the Mississippi rivers, while
Deacon Chittenden, with a farm wagon, took the horses, and,
with his eldest son and Mr. Plant, started to make their way
across the new States of Ohio, Indiana, and Illinois to Alton,
the place of destination. In the spring the families aban-
doned their plan of settling near each other, Mr. Plant
and wife returning to the East, and Mr. Clark removing to
Jacksonville, where he assisted in organizing the first Congregational church, his name standing third on the roll. He
performed a similar service in two other places where he
afterward lived. Buying a farm at Diamond Grove, near
Jacksonville, he commenced farming with all the enthusiasm

of his younger days, but after a few years gave it up, and became steward of Illinois College, then under the presidency of Edward Beecher.

"From Jacksonville he removed to Rushville, in the same State. Remaining here but a short time, he followed his eldest son, then a practicing physician, to Iowa, and afterward to Wisconsin, where his second son was engaged in mercantile business. His next removal was to Chicago with Dr. Holbrook, a son-in-law, his two sons having removed to California. In the summer of 1854 he revisited his early home, spending several weeks, and seemed to renew his youth, walking long distances as he visited one and another of his old friends, but it was as the last brightening of the flame before it expires. He returned to Chicago, and for a short time enjoyed anew his summer's pleasures in recounting them to his family. Soon, however, he began to show signs of exhausted vitality. During the early weeks of winter he sat by the fire sleeping most of the time, his strength gradually failing, until, with no appearance of disease, on the 21st of February, he quietly passed away. Mr. Clark's life was eminently a religious one. Of a cheerful temperament, he had a store of proverbs and quaint sayings by which he was wont to express a sense of thankfulness for blessings received. His principles were those of the good old Puritan sort. He dared to reverence the Sabbath when few regarded it. He began to be a consistent advocate of temperance while the use of alcoholic drinks was almost universal, and through a long and useful life was a bright example of all that is true, and loving, and of good report."

His children were:

    i. JOSEPH WASHBURN, b. Nov. 30, 1810; d. Jan. 12, 1812.

36.   ii.   JOSEPH WASHBURN, b. Jan. 19, 1813.
       iii.   MARY, b. Jan. 6, 1815; d. Dec. 13, 1815.
37.   iv.   MARY WETMORE, b. Nov. 29, 1816.
38.   v.   DENNIS WOODRUFF, b. May 27, 1819.
39.   vi.   JANE ELIZA, b. Dec. 9, 1822.
       vii.   ANNE LOUISA, b. Dec. 9, 1822, twin sister of (**39**);
              m. Oct. 18, 1842, Rev. John C. Holbrook, D.D., born
              June 7, 1808, son of John and Sarah (Knowlton)
              Holbrook. For a minute and extended notice of Dr.
              Holbrook, see *History of Brattleboro, Vt., by Henry
              Burnham*, 159.
40.   viii. LUCY ELLEN, b. May 13, 1826.
       ix.   ELNATHAN GRIDLEY, b. Feb. 28, 1828; d. Nov. 8,
              1828.

26.   GILLETT.

Huldah[5] (*Mervin,[4] John,[3] Matthew,[2] John[1]*), b. April 3,
1789; m. Dec. 30, 1823, Eri Gillett, son of Capt. Obadiah
and Hannah (Wilcox) Gillett. Eri was made a freeman
Sept. 21, 1818, and must therefore have been born as early as
1797. He died April 19, 1874. Huldah died April 16, 1881.
They lived in Avon, Conn., about one mile south of Avon
Center.

Their children were:

i.   CORNELIA, b. Jan. 27, 1825; d. Jan. 3, 1831.
ii.   HENRY CLARK, b. Feb. 5, 1827; m. May 17, 1848, Lucy
       Leavitt Hamlin, daughter of William and Harriet
       Hamlin of Litchfield, South Farms.
iii.   GEORGE FREDERICK, b. May 13, 1829; m. October, 1859,
       Catharine Gridley, baptized in West Hartford, Aug.
       12, 1832, daughter of Mark and Dorothy (Selden)
       Gridley of Farmington, Northeast District.
iv.   CORNELIA MARGARET, b. Oct. 1, 1831; m. March 22,
       1857, Jacob Levi Cline of Zoans, Prussia, son of Abra-
       ham and Eliza (Davis) Levi. The name of his god-
       father Klein was substituted for Levi at the time of his

confirmation in London, England, and has since been
Anglicized into Cline.

27.

Matthew[5] (*Dan*,[4] *John*,[3] *Matthew*,[2] *John*[1]), b. Oct. 2, 1773;
m. June 27, 1793, Rhoda North, born Feb. 10, 1776, daughter
of James and Rhoda (Judd) North, died April 19, 1840, aged
64. He m. 2d, Nov. 8, 1841, Sarah Giddings, born Oct. 24,
1789, at Preston, Conn., died July 28, 1878, at Hartford,
Conn., daughter of Solomon and Ruth (Wright) Giddings.
Matthew died Jan. 13, 1851, aged 77 (*gravestone*). Their
children were:

41.   i.   JAMES STANLEY, b. Nov. 3, 1794.
      ii.   GEORGE, b. Aug. 1, 1796; d. Feb. 15, 1803.
     iii.   LUCY, b. March 6, 1799; d. June 30, 1803.
     iv.   ABI, b. Feb. 5, 1801; d. Jan. 18, 1840.
42.   v.   DAN, b. Jan. 15, 1805.
     vi.   GEORGE, b. Aug. 18, 1807; d. Nov. 3, 1810.

The dates of the births of the children above are from
Andrews' New Britain, 325. Those of the deaths are from
gravestones.

28.

Manly[5] (*Abel*,[4] *John*,[3] *Matthew*,[2] *John*[1]), b. April 1, 1776;
m. (Nov. 9, 1797, Sarah Hart, born Nov. 9, 1778. See
Stephen Hart & His Descendants, 457), daughter of Elizur
and Sarah (Langdon) Hart. They lived in Stanley Quarter,
New Britain, where he died May 1, 1812, and his widow married
2d, Feb. 27, 1821, Martin Lee, born Oct. 10, 1778, died Jan.
21, 1841, aged 62, son of Timothy and Lucy (Camp) Lee.
Sarah died Dec. 19, 1860. The children of Manly were:

   i.   ABIGAIL JUDD, b. March 28, 1799; d. July 3, 1804.
  ii.   ELIZUR HART, b. Aug. 17, 1801; d. Dec. 6, 1824.
iii.   JULIA ABIGAIL, b. July 23, 1807; d. Feb. 1, 1813.

The dates of all the above deaths are from gravestones. Those of the births of the three children are from *Stephen Hart & His Descendants*, 457, and all others from the town records of Farmington and Southington, except as indicated.

29. ANDREWS.

Mary[3] (*Abel*,[4] *John*,[3] *Matthew*[2], *John*[1]), b. Sept. 25, 1784; m. Oct. 24, 1804, Col. Sidney Andrews of New York City, born March 8, 1780, and died Feb. 20, 1864, in Montague, Mass, son of Moses, Jr., and Elizabeth (Clark) Andrews. He was the (**23**, i) of this genealogy, was for many years a printer, lived in New York City, and was a colonel in the State militia. Mary died Dec. 29, 1862. Their children were:

i. CORNELIA ELIZABETH, b. Aug. 23, 1807; m. Oct. 11, 1848, Charles Eldridge Rogers, born March 22, 1816, son of Benjamin and Abigail (Hammond) Rogers.

ii. JOHN CLARK, b. Dec. 19, 1809; m. Jan. 22, 1832, Tirzah Ann Field, born April 27, 1809, died March 19, 1856, daughter of Robert and Martha (Hoit) Field. He m. 2d, Feb. 5, 1863, Susan P. Hayden, born Nov. 27, 1827, daughter of Cicero M. and Mary (Pendleton) Hayden. He lives in Montague City, Mass., is by trade a trunk and harness maker, and has a numerous family.

iii. MARY ABIGAIL, b. Dec. 22, 1811; m. Dec. 24, 1827, Aaron R. Burnham, who died Jan. 19, 1877, aged 75, son of Silas and Aurilla (Robbins) Burnham. She died June 5, 1873.

iv. CATHARINE JANE, b. Dec. 27, 1819; d Jan. 10, 1839, unmarried.

v. MARIA, b. Aug. 2, 1824; d. Aug. 3, 1824.

My authority for this genealogy of Mary[3] Clark is John Clark Andrews (**29**, ii) above.

30.

John[5] (*Abel*,[4] *John*,[3] *Matthew*,[2] *John*[1]), b. March 20, 1787 ; m. Aug. 26, 1812, Prudence Woodruff, born Aug. 3, 1793, daughter of Joshua and Prudence (Curtiss) Woodruff. He lived in the old house of his father and grandfather, in Stanley Quarter, New Britain, was a farmer and butcher, and established the first meat-market in New Britain. It stood at or near the intersection of Main street with the New York & New England railroad, to the north of the railroad and to the west of Main street. He served in the war of 1812 as Corporal of Capt. Dan. Deming's company in Col. Brainard's regiment, from Aug. 18 to Oct. 25, 1814, and was stationed at New London, as appears by the records of the Pension Office at Washington. He died Jan. 27, 1835, and was buried in the old cemetery of New Britain. Their children were :

    i.   JANE, b. Nov. 14, 1813 : d. Feb. 17, 1818.

43. ii. MATILDA, b. Oct. 24, 1815.

    iii. GEORGE, b. June 20, 1817 : m. Jan. 16, 1845, Sarah E. Castlen of Culloden, Georgia, born in Hanover Co., Virginia, Feb. 25, 1825, daughter of John and Eliza (Grantland) Castlen. He died July 15, 1845, at Macon, Georgia. He left no children, and his widow married Thomas Cauthron of Griffin, Georgia.

44. iv. ABEL NEWELL, b. June 12, 1819.

45. v. JOHN WOODRUFF, b. July 3, 1822.

    vi. JANE LOUISA, b. Oct. 2, 1827 : m. March 2, 1845, Deming W. Sexton, born Dec. 12, 1819, son of Walter and Nancy (Barton) Sexton. They had a child born March 24, 1846, and died the next day. She died May 25, 1846.

    vii. MARY PRUDENCE, b. Nov. 7, 1830; d. May 17, 1834.

46. viii. ELLEN AMELIA, b. Dec. 2, 1833.

The above dates are from John Woodruff Clark (**45**), from

the family bible of Prudence Clark, wife of (**30**), and from gravestones.

31.

Sylvester[5] (*Abel*,[4] *John*,[3] *Matthew*,[2] *John*[1]), b. Feb. 18, 1789; m. 1810, Hannah Hart, born Oct. 7, 1792, died Dec. 24, 1869, daughter of Asahel and Hannah (Langdon) Hart. He died in Hartford, Ct., April 18, 1829. Their children were:

    i.   LANGDON, b. June 11, 1811; d. Dec. 24, 1813.
    ii. OPHELIA, b. March 23, 1813; d. June 25, 1882.
    iii. LANGDON, b. Sept. 3, 1815; d. July 13, 1843.
    iv. JANE ADELAIDE, b. July 12, 1818; d. Jan. 7, 1820.
47. v. JAMES W., b. Sept. 14, 1820.
    vi. JANE, b. March 9, 1823.
48. vii. CHARLOTTE, b. May 13, 1825.

The above dates are from a very carefully written letter of Ophelia Clark (**31**, ii), since deceased.

32.   ADAMS.

Eliza Jane[5] (*John*,[4] *John*,[3] *Matthew*,[2] *John*[1]), b. Dec. 5, 1797; m. Nov. 1, 1817, William Henry Adams, born May, 1787; died March 31, 1865, son of John Adams of Bloomfield, N. Y. She died June 11, 1855.

Their children were:

    i.   JOHN CLARK, b. Aug. 29, 1818; graduated at Harvard college, 1839; d. Jan. 24, 1874
    ii. ELIZA JANE, b. July 5, 1820: m. Oct. 15, 1846, at Clyde, N. Y., Henry Joseph Ruggles, d. Feb. 11, 1853.
    iii. WILLIAM HENRY, b. July 16, 1822; d. Sept. 5, 1839.
    iv. JAMES BEMIS, b. Jan. 12, 1825, at Lyons, Wayne Co., N. Y.; graduated at Harvard college, 1847: studied medicine and received the degree of M.D. at the New York Medical School in 1851: d. Jan. 16, 1853, at Curacoa, West Indies, of yellow fever.

v. MARK SIBLEY, b. April 10, 1827, at Lyons, Wayne Co., N. Y.; graduated at Harvard College, 1847; d. Feb. 19, 1853, in San Francisco, Cal.

vi. EDWARD, b. Sept. 10, 1829; d. May 27, 1834.

vii. ALEXANDER DUNCAN, b. Dec. 25, 1832; m. June 19, 1856, at Lyons, Wayne Co., N. Y., Ellen Clare Hotchkiss: was a Colonel in the late war; d. Oct. 28, 1872.

viii. MARIA SIBLEY, b. Oct. 9, 1835; m. Dec. 8, 1858, Henry Joseph Ruggles, born August 1, 1813, son of Philo and Ellen (Bulkley) Ruggles. Now living at Carmanville, 161st street, N. Y.

ix. CHARLES ELIOT, b. Oct. 31, 1838; d. Jan. 11, 1866. Was Lieut. Colonel under Bissell in Mississippi in the late war.

The above dates were contributed by Mrs. Alexander Duncan Adams, widow of (32, vii.) See also *N. E. Hist. and Gen. Register*, vii, 372.

33. SIBLEY.

Maria Green[1] (*John*,[4] *John*,[3] *Matthew*,[2] *John*[1]), b. Jan., 1802; m. Nov., 1821, Mark Hopkins Sibley, born 1796 in Great Barrington, Mass., removed to Canandaigua, N. Y., in 1814, and became a distinguished lawyer; was in the N. Y. Assembly in 1835 and 1836; in Congress in 1837–9; State senator in 1840–1, and elected county judge and surrogate of Ontario county in 1847; died at Canandaigua, N. Y., Sept. 8, 1852. His wife died May, 1876. Their children were:

i. MARY HOPKINS, b. Sept., 1822; m. Sept., 1844, John Ganson, born in Leroy, N. Y.; graduated at Harvard College in 1839; removed to Buffalo at the age of 30; was a prominent lawyer, and in 1862–3 a State senator; died at Buffalo Sept. 28, 1874, aged 57. His wife is living.

ii. JOHN CLARK, b. May 6, 1824; m. Nov., 1856, Mary Y. Gibson, daughter of Henry B. Gibson of Canandaigua, N. Y. She died October, 1865.

iii. EMILY WARD, b. October 28, 1848; d. October 20, 1856.

8

The above dates are from *American Biographical Notes, by
F. B. Hough*, 155 and 362, and a letter of Mrs. M. H. Ganson (33, i.).

34.

Henry White[5] (*Ornan*,[5] *Mervin*,[4] *John*,[3] *Matthew*,[2] *John*[1]),
b. Feb. 23, 1807 ; m. Oct. 21, 1832, Emily Rowena Stanley,
born Sept. 11, 1810, and died March 10, 1869, in Dubuque,
Iowa, daughter of Cyrus and Abigail (Lee) Stanley. He
died in Cleveland, Ohio, Sept. 6, 1872. The following obituary notice was published in a Cleveland newspaper soon after
his death :

"We have published the fact of the prostration on
Wednesday last of Mr. Henry W. Clark by paralysis. That
gentleman lingered in an unconscious state until Friday afternoon, when he died. His age was sixty-eight, the place of
his nativity New Britain, Conn., and he has been a resident
of Cleveland since about 1833. Latterly Mr. Clark has spent
the most of his time at Dubuque, but up to a few years past he
was among the most active, most liberal, and most valuable
of Cleveland's citizens. Mr. Clark commenced business here
in the dry goods line under the firm name of H. W. and M.
Clark, having a small store on Superior street near where the
Johnson house now stands. Subsequently he became member
of the firms of Clark and Raymond and Clark and Morgan.
withdrawing from merchandise some fifteen years since, when
he became interested largely and intimately in the Cleveland
and Pittsburg Railroad project.

"The deceased was one of the original members of the
Second Presbyterian Church, and was one of the few who
brought to completion the edifice on Superior street still
occupied by that society, and always was a generous, laborious,
and constant friend of that church, with whose name his

own is closely allied, and whose memory will be cherished
while any of the present members of that society remain.

" But to measure the full merits of the deceased one needed
to cross the threshold of his old home. Mr. Clark had no
children, yet himself and wife—the latter having preceded
him, and by a sudden death, too, a few years since—had upon
their hearts the children of others, and their roof was never
too narrow to shelter those dear to them. It was in deeds of
beautiful charity that the memory of the late Mr. and Mrs.
Clark blossoms so luxuriantly in the dust. They never wearied
in giving, and while it is sad to think that a man always so
active, always so cheerful, always so just and liberal, should
not of the fortune he once possessed leave large bequests to
those he adopted, still he does leave a legacy to friends that
is above price and that shall also prove to him a treasure laid
up in heaven."

35.

Mervin[5] (*Ornan*,[5] *Mervin*,[4] *John*,[3] *Matthew*,[2] *John*[1]), baptized and probably born Jan., 1812; m. July 1, 1839, in
Cleveland, Ohio, Caroline Guptil, born May 22, 1822, in
Cleveland, and died April 4, 1847, in Milwaukee, Wisconsin,
daughter of John H. and Lucy (White) Guptil. He married,
second, Nov. 6, 1849, Mary Jane Tharp, born Jan. 10, 1828,
daughter of Amariah and Elizabeth (Hines) Tharp. His
widow married, second, April 16, 1856, Jeduthan Hopkins, son of Matthew and Lucy Hopkins of Rensselaer,
Indiana. In early life Mr. Clark was a clerk in the
well-known dry goods store of Julius Catlin in Hartford,
Conn., and afterwards in that of A. M. Collins in the same
city. Subsequently he entered into a partnership with his
brother Henry W. Clark in the dry goods business on Superior street, in Cleveland, Ohio. He afterwards, in the fall of

1846, established himself in the same business in Milwaukee, Wisconsin, and still later in Rensselaer, Indiana. In this latter place his health rapidly failed, and going east for a little rest he visited his sister Sarah in New Britain, Conn., and there died June 27, 1854, aged 42. His remains are interred in the southeastern part of the New Britain cemetery.

Children by his first wife :

    i. ALMIRA, b. May 11, 1840; m. Jan. 3, 1872, in New Britain, Ct., George Sumner Brittain, born June 1, 1844, son of Henry and Mary L. (Brandon) Brittain.

49. ii. MARIA, b. April 22, 1841.

50. iii. MERVIN, b. Nov. 5, 1843.

    iv. THOMAS STANLEY, b. May 12, 1845; baptized by the name Oliver Stanley. Is a bookseller in Watertown, Wisconsin.

Children by second wife :

    v. LUCY SUTTON, b. Aug. 27, 1850; d. March 3, 1852.

    vi. HENRY, b. May 13, 1852; d. June 19, 1855.

36.

Joseph Washburn (*Abraham,[5] Mervin,[4] John,[3] Matthew,[2] John[1]*), b. Jan. 19, 1813; m. Sept. 28, 1837,[*] Lucy Ashman Hooker, born Sept. 28, 1812, died April 17, 1839, daughter of William and Octavia (Hale) Hooker of Westfield, Mass. He married second, April 10, 1842, Jane Wells Fessenden,

---

*This date is interesting as illustrating a conflict of testimony, either side of which taken alone, would seem proved beyond doubt. Doct. Clark wrote in his family bible that he was married on the 29th of Sept., which was on Friday. Members of his family, in particular two sisters now living, remember that he insisted on being married on Friday purposely, to show his contempt of popular superstition, and that he often alluded to the fact in after life. On the other hand, William Hooker, father of Mrs. Clark, entered the date in his bible as the 28th. The official record of the town clerk of Westfield has it the 28th, and there is a tradition that Mrs. Clark was married on her birthday.

born August 24, 1815, daughter of Joseph and Sibbel Lane
(Holbrook) Fessenden, and sister of Rev. Thomas K. Fessenden of Farmington, Ct. Dr. Clark died Dec. 17, 1878. The
following sketch of his life and deserved tribute to his memory is contributed by his niece, Milicent W. Shinn, No. 10, v,
of this genealogy.

"It was not an uncommon saying among those who knew
Dr. Clark, that he was 'the most perfect Puritan in San
Francisco.' Clear-headed, silent and intense in his affections,
flawlessly upright and fair, utterly loyal to an obligation, unwavering in religious belief,—he did approach very nearly the
genuine Puritan ideal, through an eventful life. His early
years in Farmington were strongly under the influence of his
mother—an influence that lasted to a marked extent through
his life. His early schooling in the district school, and the
Farmington Academy, was followed by a time in the Westfield (Mass.) Academy, where he was prepared for college.
In 1830, the year that he entered college, his father moved
to New Haven, and thence, a year later, to Jacksonville, Illinois. The family was in pecuniary difficulty, and though
Joseph had all the help his family could give, and did all he
could for himself, (he had taught school before entering college,) he was obliged to leave at the end of three years. He
returned however in 1835, after having earned money by
teaching, and studied medicine at the same time with Dr.
Henry of Springfield, Illinois. In 1837 he graduated from
the Medical School. His aspiration had been for the ministry: he did not think himself well adapted to it, but in laying aside his hopes of entering that profession, he deliberately
devoted himself to lay service for the church instead. Dr.
Clark began practice at Rushville, Ill.; thence removed to
Rockingham, Iowa; thence to Parkhurst, Iowa; and thence,

in 1842, to Platteville, Wis. From the time he began practice, Dr. Clark (himself just married) took upon himself the
whole burden of the family, for his father gave up active life
about this time, and the young doctor became the responsible
head of the family, until it was scattered by the marriage of
his younger brother and sisters. He was everywhere the
tireless friend of church and school. The Academy at Platteville (now a State Normal School), owed its existence to him;
he and his brother fairly set glass and quarried stone for the
new building. Under his care the school was made a very
unusual one for the region. The country was new and rough,
and in Dr. Clark's large practice (of twenty or thirty miles),
his life included many adventures—dangers by flood and
field, encounters with violent men, ludicrous incidents among
the rough people of the country, discomforts and difficulties
—that would have been impossible in New England. He
was at this time an active and daring young man, who rather
courted than avoided dangers.

"In the spring of 1850 Dr. Clark left Platteville to cross
the plains to California; he went with a mule team, by way of
St. Jo, and Fort Atchinson. He never traveled on Sunday ;
whatever danger of Indians there might be, the wagons belonging to his party always stopped on Sunday, letting the
rest of the train push on in their eagerness to reach California ; and it always came out that his teams, refreshed by a
day's rest, overtook the train before the next Sabbath. His
outfit had been planned with so much foresight and care that
he accomplished the journey with far less risk and privation
than was usual. As he approached Marysville, the first point
at which he could expect letters, some one overtook him, who
had passed through Platteville, and told him that there had
been sickness and death in his family. Dr. Clark had

exchanged his mules for oxen at Salt Lake; unable to endure the suspense of their slow pace, he left his team and walked to Marysville, some sixty miles, walking all night, without food or rest. It was after the terrible exertion and anxiety of this walk that the heart-disease first appeared which ended his life.

"At Georgetown, fairly among the mines, Dr. Clark went into trade with his brother-in-law, Elias Gill, and prospered. In 1852 he went back and brought his wife and children to San Francisco; a year or two later, his mother and a sister, now Mrs. Sanford of Oakland, Cal., joined him: in 1856, his youngest sister, Mrs. Shinn, came to Niles, Cal.; and a third sister, Mrs. Holbrook, and his brother Dennis have both lived for a short time in California; so that even after his removal to the western coast, Dr. Clark remained the center of the family group.

"The quarter century of his life in San Francisco was occupied in mercantile pursuits and filled with the utmost devotion to the public good, especially through the church and like channels. His business life was blameless; he was indispensable to his church (the First Congregational, that of Dr. A. L. Stone). In 1862-3, he served in the legislature of California; his uncompromising standard of honor there, though it must have stood sometimes in the way of party schemes, is spoken of still with uniform admiration by all who knew him in that capacity. In the autumn of 1878 a neglected cold produced a congestion of the lungs that, joined with the old heart disease, brought him to the grave. His thought and care for others never failed through his long sickness; on the last day of his life, when his strength had already ebbed so low that his friends expected the end almost hourly, when his senses were failing and his mind wandering,

he insisted on being raised in bed, given his spectacles, and
on going over the church accounts with the gentleman to
whom he had transferred them; and did go over them from
beginning to end, clearly and correctly, recalling his failing
mind by an incredible effort, that probably shortened his few
remaining hours. The incident was strikingly characteristic
of his most dominant trait,—an intense desire to fulfill to the
very utmost any obligation that lay upon him.

"'He was a man of singular fidelity to his ideals of personal duty. These ideals were high. They covered all that
his capacity and opportunity brought within his sphere of
witnessing and doing.' * To neglect or evade any duty would
be to his mind shame and sin; to do it, no merit, simply a
matter of course. He was, therefore, so unassuming that his
Puritanic principles and habits, kept untarnished through all
his western life, never won him dislike or ridicule; he was
always respected, even by men who cared nothing for his
creed. From the time when he learned his catechism beside
his mother's spinning-wheel in a Farmington farm-house, and
guided his blind grandfather every Sunday to his seat in the
Farmington church, through all his school and college life,
his medical practice in the wild West, and his long business
life in San Francisco, he was a boy and man of peculiarly
blameless life and character."

His children were:

> i. WILLIAM HOOKER, b. April 11, 1839, in Rushville,
> Ill., according to Dr. Clark's bible, but a letter from
> him to his father-in-law dated April 12, 1839, says,
> "This morning, about 2 o'clock, William Hooker
> Clark made his entry into this place"; d. May 6,
> 1839, at Rushville.

---

* Obituary in *Congregationalist*.—Dr. A. L. Stone.

ii. Lucy Hooker, b. April 1, 1844, in Platteville, Wis.;
m. May 5, 1868, Henry Baldwin Tichenor, born Nov.
8, 1824, in Newark, N. J., son of Nehemiah and
Eunice (Brown) Tichenor. They reside in San Francisco. He has a very extensive lumber business, own-
ing a good many miles of red-wood forest along the
Navarro river in Mendocino Co., at the mouth of
which river his saw-mill is located. He owns also a
few schooners engaged in Alaska fisheries.

iii. Mary Elizabeth. b. Dec. 11. 1846, in Platteville:
d. May 31, 1850, in Platteville.

51. iv. Joseph Fessenden, b. Oct. 31, 1848, in Platteville.

v. Mary. b. May 28. 1854, in San Francisco; d. Aug.,
1854.

vi. Edward Holbrook, b. June 18, 1859, in San Francisco; d. Jan. 25, 1860.

37. GILL.

Mary Wetmore[5] (*Abraham*,[5] *Mervin*,[4] *John*,[3] *Matthew*,[2]
John[1]), b. Nov. 29, 1816, in Farmington, m. Nov. 1, 1837, at
Rushville, Ill., Elias Gill of Hartford, Conn., born Nov. 16,
1808, in Middletown, Conn., died Sept. 19, 1880, in Oakland,
Cal., son of Samuel and Jane (Watkinson) Gill. She died
April 2, 1845, in Platteville, Wis., and Elias Gill married
second, his cousin, Jane Watkinson, born Feb. 22, 1827, in
New York city, daughter of William and Elizabeth (McCall)
Watkinson of Middletown.

Children by first marriage:

i. Ellen, b. Jan. 18, 1839, at Rockingham, Iowa: d. Sept.
20, 1845, at Platteville. Wisconsin.

ii. George, b. Aug. 2, 1844, at Platteville; d. April 26,
1845, at the same place.

Children by second marriage:

iii. Mary, b.——; d. in Milwaukee.

iv. Emily, b. June 4, 1857.

9

v.   WILLIAM WATKINSON, b. Nov. 20, 1859, in San Francisco.
vi. ELIZABETH, b. July 3, 1861, in Petaluma, Cal.

38.

Dennis Woodruff (*Abraham,*[5] *Mervin,*[4] *John,*[3] *Matthew,*[2] *John*[1]), b. May 27, 1819, in Farmington ; m. Aug. 22, 1850, Mary Caroline Hubbs, born April 1, 1819, in Portland, Maine, daughter of Alexander and Mary (Lowell) Hubbs.

The following statement of the principal facts of his life was contributed by a member of the family :

"Mr. Clark was born in Farmington, May 27, 1819. Leaving that town with his father's family, when about eleven years old, he spent twenty-two years in the West, finally locating in Portland, Maine, where he is now living. Going West in 1831, he had no opportunity for more than a common school education. His business education commenced as a clerk in the book-store of Mr. Jeremy L. Cross, in New Haven, Ct. After removing West he was clerk for merchants in Naples and Jacksonville, Illinois, and St. Louis, Missouri. Leaving St. Louis in 1845, he made his first venture in business at Rockingham, Iowa, but afterwards went to Platteville, Wisconsin, where he engaged in mining and mercantile pursuits until 1852. While living in Platteville he united, March 10, 1844, with the Presbyterian church, and August 22, 1850, was married in Portland, Maine, to Miss Hubbs, daughter of Capt. Alexander Hubbs. In 1852 a partnership was formed with his brother, Dr. J. W. Clark, and brother-in-law, Mr. Elias Gill, under the firm name of Gill, Clark & Co., for trading in California. Here his next two years were spent in San Francisco and Sacramento. Returning in 1854, he located in Portland, and has for twenty-eight years been engaged in the ice business in that city, for nineteen years carrying on

the business alone, taking a partner in 1873, and organizing
the business into a joint stock company in 1882. THE CLARK
& CHAPLIN ICE CO., of which he is the president, represents
a large and well-established business, cutting, storing, and
shipping ice in large quantities, in addition to the local city
trade. He has also been connected with other business en-
terprises. He was treasurer of the Leeds & Farmington R.
R. Co. from December, 1869, until it was sold to the Maine
Central R. R.; afterward a director of the Portland &
Ogdensburg R. R. in 1872, while the road was being con-
structed through the mountains and until it was completed
and the cars were running through Crawford Notch, resigning
in 1879. In 1873 he was chosen a director, and afterwards
president, of the Portland Water Company, which position
he now occupies."

Children:

i.   MARY MILICENT. b. July 19, 1851; d. Sept. 1, 1854, in
     Chicago.
ii. ALEXANDER HUBBS, b. Feb. 26, 1853; d. Aug. 2, 1853.
iii. EMMA WASHBURN, b. March 26, 1855; m. Dec. 29, 1881,
     George Washington Percy, born July 5, 1847, in Bath,
     Maine, son of Josiah and Beulah (Bowker) Percy.
iv. ISABELLA TYLER, b. Nov. 26, 1857.
v.   MERVIN WASHBURN, b. July 27, 1861.

39. SANFORD.

Jane Eliza[6] (*Abraham*,[5] *Mervin*,[4] *John*,[3] *Matthew*,[2] *John*[1]),
b. Dec. 9, 1822, in Farmington; m. Jan. 26, 1858, in San
Francisco, Edmund Philo Sanford, born Aug. 25, 1826, in
Newark, N. J.; d. Feb. 14, 1880, son of Philo and Martha
(Druce) Sanford. The following extracts from the sermon
delivered in the First Congregational Church of Oakland, Cal.,
at his funeral, give the most prominent facts of his life:

" Being removed with his parents, while he was yet in his infancy, from Newark, Mr. Sanford's boyhood and school life were spent in Wrentham, Mass., not far from the ancestral home. Subsequently his family removed again; this time to Hallowell, in the State of Maine. . . . . From Hallowell he came to California, arriving here in 1850, residing chiefly in San Francisco until 1858. In January of that year he was married to Miss Jane Eliza Clark, and in August following he established his home in Oakland, where from that date to his death he was engaged in business."

Children :

   i. EDMUND CLARK, b. Nov. 10, 1859, at Oakland, Cal.
   ii. MARTHA LEWIS, b. Sept. 30, 1861, at Oakland, Cal.

10.   SHINN.

Lucy Ellen (*Abraham,*[6] *Merrin,*[4] *John,*[3] *Matthew,*[2] *John,*[1]) b. May 13, 1826, in Farmington, Conn.; m. Nov. 26, 1846, in Platteville, Wisconsin, James Shinn, born Sept. 29, 1807, in Salem, Ohio, son of Thomas and Rebecca (Daniels) Shinn. He now lives in Niles, California, and has an extensive nursery of fruit and ornamental trees. He was previously married, Nov., 1828, to Mary Sebrell, born July 29, 1800, died Oct. 16, 1845, at Platteville, Wisconsin, daughter of Joseph and Rebecca (Jones) Sebrell.

Children of James and Mary Shinn :

   i. ELI, b. Sept. 15, 1829 ; d. Aug. 15, 1843.
   ii. REBECCA DANIELS, b. Nov. 8, 1831 ; d. July 28, 1854.
   iii. HANNAH BRANTINGHAM, b. April 19, 1833. Living in Texas.
   iv. MARY ANN, b. March 16, 1835 ; d. about 1868.
   v. WILLIAM HENRY, b. Sept. 27, 1837 ; d. about 1863.

Children of James and Lucy Ellen (Clark) Shinn:

i. ELLEN MARY, b. Sept. 14, 1847, in Platteville, Wisconsin; d. Aug. 18, 1848, in Dubuque, Iowa.

ii. EDWIN, b. Sept. 28, 1848, in Dubuque, Iowa; d. Sept. 30, 1848.

iii. CHARLES HOWARD, b. April 29, 1852, in Round Rock, Texas. Is sub-editor of the San Francisco Bulletin.

iv. ANNE HOLBROOK, b. May 6, 1856, in Round Rock, Texas; d. Jan. 13, 1878, in Niles, Cal.

v. MILICENT WASHBURN, b. April 15, 1858, in Niles, Cal. Is editor of the Californian.

vi. JOSEPH CLARK, b. Jan. 15, 1861, in Niles, Cal.

vii. LUCY ELLEN, b. Sept. 5, 1863: d. Dec. 13, 1873, in Niles, Cal.

41.

James Stanley[5] (*Matthew,*[5] *Dan,*[4] *John,*[3] *Matthew,*[2] *John*[1].) b. Nov. 3, 1794; m. Oct. 9, 1817, Amanda Rowe, born (Oct. 16, 1796, died Jan. 10, 1864, *W. S. Gridley authority,*) daughter of Isaiah and Mary (Gridley) Rowe. He died Feb. 7, 1820, and his widow Amanda married May 10, 1826, Chauncey Ives of Bristol, Conn.

Child of James Stanley and Amanda (Rowe) Clark:

52. i. MARY ANTOINETTE, b. Sept. 26, 1819.

42.

Dan[5] (*Matthew,*[5] *Dan,*[4] *John,*[3] *Matthew,*[2] *John*[1]), b. Jan. 15, 1805, on Clark Hill in Stanley Quarter, New Britain: m. Sept. 4, 1827, Mary Whittlesey, born Sept. 12, 1809, daughter of David and Rebecca (Smalley) Whittlesey. He lived for many years in a house now (1882) owned and occupied by Joshua B. Brewer, on the east side of the Stanley Quarter road, near the present northern limit of the town of New Britain, on land formerly within the limits of the town of Farmington, but taken from the latter town and added to

New Britain on petition to the Legislature by **Dan Clark** and
others in the year 1859. He was a farmer, a colonel of
cavalry in the State militia of Connecticut, and, during the
latter part of his life in New Britain, a noted mover of buildings. He removed to Boonsboro, Boone Co., Iowa, in the
year 1868, where he has been a deacon, a Sunday-school
superintendent, and is still, though far advanced in years,
engaged in the business of moving buildings.

His children:

    i. JAMES STANLEY, b. April 20, 1829; d. June 20,
          1839.

53. ii. REBECCA SMALLEY, b. Feb. 8, 1832.

54. iii. WILLIAM WHITTLESEY, b. March 19, 1834.

    iv. FRANCES FEDORA, b. Feb. 28, 1836: d. April 3,
          1837.

55. v. ELBERT CORNELIUS, b. July 30, 1838.

56. vi. FRANCES FEDORA, b. March 15, 1841.

    vii. JAMES ELIPHALET, b. May 18, 1843; d. Oct. 25,
          1844.

57. viii. MATTHEW HENRY, b. Aug. 8, 1846.

58. ix. ADRIAN IVES, b. Sept. 15, 1849.

The above dates were obtained from William Whittlesey
Clark (**54**). See also *Andrews' New Britain*, and New
Britain gravestones.

43. WARNER.

Matilda (*John,⁵ Abel,⁴ John,³ Matthew,² John¹*), b. Oct.
24, 1815: m. Dec. 14, 1836, Charles Alexander Warner, born
April 19, 1811, at Troy, N. Y.: died June 28, 1868, in New
Britain, Conn., son of Willard and Betsey (Burke) Warner
of Chester, Vt. He was a jeweler in New Britain. She
died Aug. 31, 1880.

Their child:

i. WILLIAM ADOLPHUS, b. April 10, 1838; d. Nov. 1, 1843.

The above dates are from the family Bible of Prudence, widow of John Clark (30), and from gravestones in New Britain.

44.

Abel Newell (*John,⁵ Abel,⁴ John,³ Matthew,² John¹*), b. June 12, 1819; m. April 27, 1840, Emily Isabella Braddock, born Dec. 7, 1821, daughter of John and Emily (Wells) Braddock. He died in Hartford, Ct., March 25, 1867. The following obituary notice was published in the Hartford Courant, of which paper he had been an editor and proprietor:

"Abel N. Clark has ceased to suffer. He died yesterday afternoon, shortly after three o'clock, in the forty-eighth year of his life.

" His long connection with this journal, and his extensive acquaintance with newspaper men and with a large majority of our readers, justify us in giving an outline of his life and character. He came to this city at an early age from New Britain, his native village, and was for some years in business here as a merchant. Being unsuccessful in his business he entered the COURANT office, when it was under the control of Mr. John L. Boswell, as book-keeper and general business manager. From that time to this (about twenty years) he has identified himself with the interests of the COURANT office. He was a man who always found something to do, and kept doing it early and late. His industry was one prominent trait in his character, and his fidelity to every trust and every duty, large or small, was another. He always took the laboring oar, and never shirked anything. That habit gave him the entire confidence of his friends, who knew that anything that depended upon him or his exertions might be safely counted upon as being as good as done. He has probably done more party work, in a quiet and unobtrusive way, than

any other individual in this State. All the details about
printing and distributing tickets, getting returns of elections,
circulating circulars, etc., etc., were left to him for many
years. His general health had been so excellent, that in the
thirteen years that the writer of this notice had been associ-
ated with him he had never been absent from the office for
more than a half day at a time. But in the fall of 1865 he
was prostrated with a bilious fever, which hung about him,
so that, March 3, 1866, he sailed for Savannah, being at that
time, as he observed to the writer, ' Sick only in my legs, and
with a sore spot on my cheek.' But that sore spot continu-
ing to trouble him, he returned from the South, and on the
21st of April underwent what proved to be a most serious
operation, at the hands of Dr. Carnochan, of New York, for
scrofulous cancer. Everything that surgical skill, seconded
by the most faithful nursing, could do, was done; but the
disease proved so malignant as to be utterly uncontrollable
and after more than eleven months of anguish unutterable,
death came to his relief. Mr. CLARK's cheerful courage in
undergoing the operation was such as to extort professional
comment, and his sufferings throughout were borne without
repining. His mind was clear and cheerful, and he looked
unflinchingly upon death, and the life beyond the grave. His
vitality and his tenacity of his usual habits was such that he
took to his bed only the day before he was relieved from suf-
fering.

" He leaves a widow and three sons. His pecuniary matters are in comfortable shape.

" So passes from among us one of our most respected citizens, and one of the most generally known newspaper men in
the country.

" His funeral took place from the First Baptist church Wednesday afternoon."

His children :

59. i.   WILLIAM BRADDOCK, b. June 29, 1841.
60. ii.   CHARLES LeRoy, b. Feb. 11, 1843.
    iii. CLARA EMILY, b. May 7, 1847 ; d. Nov. 19, 1848.
61. iv.   GEORGE NEWELL, b. Nov. 12, 1851.

The dates relating to the above family were obtained from William Braddock Clark (59).

45.

John Woodruff (*John,* *Abel,* *John,* *Matthew,* *John'*), b. July 3, 1822; m. April 7, 1858, Caroleen Beckley, born in Berlin, Ct., July 27, 1829, daughter of Orin and Harriet (Patterson) Beckley. Mr. CLARK gives the compiler of this genealogy the following very concise and modest account of his life:

" Born and lived in the home of his father until fifteen years of age, after which lived four years in Buffalo, N. Y., one year in Hartford, Ct., seven years in Macon, Ga., twelve years in New York City, four years in New Britain and Kensington, moving thence to Mt. Vernon, N. Y., in 1865, where he continues to reside. His business has carried him into every State in the Union, save one, and into nearly every territory, and that without accident by rail, steamboat, or stage."

His children :

 i.   MARY ELEANOR, b. Jan. 18, 1859, in Brooklyn, N. Y.; m. Oct. 8, 1879, Rev. Mancius Holmes Hutton, D.D., born Oct. 13, 1837, son of Rev. Mancius S. Hutton, D.D., and Gertrude (Holmes) Hutton.
 ii. EDWARD HERBERT, b. Nov. 18, 1860, in New Britain, Ct.

10

iii. CAROLEEN BECKLEY, b. June 12, 1862, in Kensington, Conn.

iv. JOHN HILLARD, b. Nov. 30, 1863, in Kensington, Conn.; d. Oct. 28, 1864.

Authority for above dates, John Woodruff Clark (45).

46. EVEREST.

Ellen Amelia[6] (*John*,[5] *Abel*,[4] *John*,[3] *Matthew*,[2] *John*[1]), b. Dec. 2, 1833; m. April 16, 1856, Cornelius Everest, born March 3, 1821, son of Rev. Cornelius Bradford Everest and Abby (Gold) Everest. He lives at No. 1428 Spruce street, Philadelphia, and is by profession a teacher of music.

Children:

i. DEWITT CLINTON, b. Aug. 1, 1861.

ii. NELLIE WARNER, b. May 14, 1864.

Authority for above dates, Cornelius Everest, Esq.

47.

James Webster[6] (*Sylvester*,[5] *Abel*,[4] *John*,[3] *Matthew*,[2] *John*[1]), b. Sept. 14, 1820; m. Dec. 14, 1847, Mary Elizabeth Varrell of Portsmouth, N. H., daughter of Hall and N. Martin Varrell. She died Oct. 30, 1857, when he married second, Sept. 6, 1864, Frances Boardman Webster of Hartford, born Feb. 6, 1829, daughter of William and Fanny (Boardman) Webster.

Children:

62. i. CHARLES H., b. Aug. 25, 1850.

63. ii. ANNIE MEDORA, b. Sept. 4, 1852.

64. iii. BELLE V., b. Aug. 26, 1855.

Authority for above dates, Charles H. Clark (62).

48. HOYT.

Charlotte[6] (*Sylvester*,[5] *Abel*,[4] *John*,[3] *Matthew*,[2] *John*[1]), b. May 13, 1825; m. Aug. 20, 1849, Franklin Comstock

Hoyt of Danbury, born April, 1827, son of Deacon Lewis
Stevens and Eliza (Clark) Hoyt.

Children:

i.   FREDERICK HART. b. Jan. 4, 1851: d. Oct. 5, 1868.
ii. ELIZABETH CLARK, b. Nov. 11, 1854.
iii. MARY FRANCES, b. May 25, 1858.
iv. CHARLOTTE LE JUNE, b. July 1, 1860.
v.   JESSE FRANKLIN, b. Aug. 16, 1864.
vi. ANNE MARIA, b. Aug. 14, 1866.

Authority for above dates. Ophelia Clark (**31**, ii).

49.   GAY.

Maria[6] (*Mervin*,[5] *Ornan*,[4] *Mervin*,[3] *John*,[3] *Matthew*,[2] *John*[1]),
b. April 22. 1841, in Cleveland. Ohio: m. Oct. 16, 1862. in
Farmington. Conn., Julius Gay. the compiler of this Genealogy. b. Feb. 15, 1834, son of Fisher and Lucy (Thomson)
Gay.

Children:

i.   MARIA, b. and d. May 20, 1866.
ii. FLORENCE THOMSON. b. July 17, 1867.
iii. LUCY CAROLINE, b. Dec. 27. 1868: d. May 29, 1869.
iv. MABEL WARNER. b. Jan. 30, 1875: d. May 1. 1880.

50.

Mervin[6] (*Mervin*,[5] *Ornan*,[4] *Mervin*,[3] *John*,[3] *Matthew*,[2]
John[1]), b. Nov. 5, 1843, in Cleveland, Ohio; d. Nov. 30. 1864.
The following biographical sketch is from the History of the
Seventh Ohio Regiment, by Major George L. Wood, 1865:

"On a gloomy night in May, 1861, when the wind was
howling in fitful gusts, and the rain pouring down in merci-
less rapidity, the writer was awakened by the stentorian voice
of the adjutant in front of the tent, followed by an order that
Lieutenant ——— would report for guard-duty. After wading

half-knee deep in mud and water, narrowly escaping a cold
bath in an over-friendly ditch, I arrived at the headquarters
of the guard. Soon after my arrival, a boy reported to me
for duty as sergeant of the guard, a position no less responsible than my own. At first I felt that, on such a fearful
night, I needed more than a boy to assist me in the perform-
ance of my task. His form was fragile ; his face was smooth
as that of a girl, and in the dim, shadowy light of a camp-
fire struggling against the heavy rain, I took him to be about
fifteen years of age. We immediately entered into conversa-
tion, and between admiration and surprise, the rain was
forgotten. and the moments sped so rapidly that it was near-
ing the time to change the guard. But my boy companion had
forgotten nothing, and as the moment arrived, he called in
the relief. As he moved among those sturdy warriors it
occurred to me that I had never before met a boy who was at
the same time a man—a brave, prudent, reliable man. All
night he did his duty, and when we parted in the morning
I both loved and admired him. This was my first meeting
with Colonel Clark.

"Mervin Clark was a native of Ohio, having been born in
the city of Cleveland in 1843. When but three years of age
his mother died, and at the age of nine his surviving parent,
leaving him an orphan. He was now taken into the family
of Henry W. Clark. an uncle, where he found a home, and
kind friends, during the remainder of his life.

"The flash of the last gun at Sumter had hardly died away,
when he enrolled himself as a private in Captain DeVilliers'
company, at the same time declaring that he would, by no
act of his, leave the service of his country, until rebels in
arms were met and subdued. How well he kept that pledge,
it is the office of this brief sketch to show.

" He left Camp Dennison as an orderly-sergeant, and during the trying marches and skirmishes in Western Virginia, won a commission. Arriving in the East, he was made a first-lieutenant. At the battle of Winchester, he surprised and delighted every one who saw him. When the bullets flew thickest, he stepped on to the brink of the hill, over which our men were firing, and, with revolver in hand, took part in the strife. His captain seeing his danger, directed him to get behind a tree which stood close by. He obeyed orders, but with his back to the tree and his face to the foe. At the battle of Cedar Mountain he commanded a company, and during that fearful day, led his men with great bravery. At last, when the order was given to retreat, he mistook it for an order to charge, and, with a dozen men, dashed at the double line of a whole brigade of rebels. It was not until an officer of authority conveyed the true order to him, that he would withdraw. He now took part in all the battles in which his regiment was engaged in the East, except Antietam. When the regiment left for the West, he accompanied it and soon after took part in the battles of Lookout Mountain, Mission Ridge. Taylor's Ridge, and the series of engagements taking place while with Sherman. Before his term of service expired, he was made a captain and commanded his company on its homeward march. He was soon after mustered out with his company. He now sought quiet and rest at his home, giving no evidence of an intention to again enter the service. But before he had been at home many weeks, he surprised and disappointed his friends by enlisting as a private in the regular army. His fame, however, was too wide-spread in Ohio to suffer him to re-enter the service as a private. Governor Brough had already selected him for promotion, and when learning of his enlistment in the regular

service, procured an order for his discharge, and immediately
appointed him lieutenant-colonel of the One Hundred and
Eighty-Third Regiment, then about to enter the field. He
had now come of age, November 5th, and on the 8th of November, cast his first vote ; on the 12th, he received his commission : and on the 15th he left for the front. His regiment
joined the army of General Thomas, on its retreat before the
rebel forces under Hood. On the 30th of November, the
regiment was engaged in the terrible battle of Franklin.
During the engagement the regiment was ordered to charge
the enemy's works. The color-bearer was soon shot down,
when Clark seized the colors, and calling to his men, ' Who
will follow me to retake these works?' mounted the rebel
works and immediately fell, a minnie ball having passed
through his head. Every effort was made to take his body
from the field, but to no purpose, and the ' boy officer ' was
wrapped in his blanket and buried on the field of his fame,
to be finally removed by careful hands, when the earth had
covered every vestige of the strife in its friendly bosom.''

51.

Joseph Fessenden (*Joseph Washburn,* *Abraham,* *Mervin,* *John,* *Matthew,*² *John*¹), b. Oct. 31, 1848, in Platteville,
Wisconsin : m. Nov. 4, 1874, Ellen Jane Dwyer, born Nov.
24, 1856 : died April 11, 1880, daughter of David and Julia
Calista Dwyer. He now lives in San Francisco, Cal.

His child :

i. LUELLA FESSENDEN, b. March 14, 1877.

52. MALLORY.

Mary Antoinette (*James Stanley,* *Matthew,* *Dan,* *John,*
*Matthew,*² *John*¹), b. Sept. 26, 1819 ; m. first, May 7, 1840,

David Sheldon Mallory, born April 16, 1818, in Montague, N.
J., died Dec. 30, 1848, son of Ransom and Lucy (Candee)
Mallory; m. second, August 28, 1869, Adrian R. Wadsworth
of Farmington, Ct., born March 12, 1815, son of Thomas H.
and Elizabeth (Rowe) Wadsworth. They are now living at
" The Sycamores," Norbeck P. O., Montgomery Co., Md.

Children :

   i. JAMES STANLEY, b. Nov. 11, 1841 ; m. Nov. 11, 1878,
      Sophia Bache Abert.

   ii. JOHN SHELDON, b. Aug. 28, 1848 : m. Oct. 1872, Helen
      Carpenter.

The above dates, with the exception of that of her birth,
were furnished by Mrs. Wadsworth. See also *Candee Genealogy by Charles C. Baldwin,* 55.

53.   PECK.

Rebecca Smalley (*Dan,⁶ Matthew,⁵ Dan,⁴ John,³ Matthew,²
John¹*), b. Feb. 8, 1832 : m. Dec. 14, 1854, James Gorham
Peck, born May 28, 1831, at Pompey, N. Y., son of Nehe-
miah and Martha (Scoville) Peck. They now live in New
Britain, Ct.

Their children :

   i. CHARLES SCOVILLE, b. Oct. 19, 1855, in Farmington, Ct.;
      d. Aug. 22, 1861, in Durant, Iowa.

   ii. MARTHA ELIZABETH, b. March 17, 1858, in Farming-
      ton, Ct.

   iii. JAMES STANLEY, b. June 6, 1864, in New Britain, Ct.

   iv. FREDERICK WHITTLESEY, b. Oct. 28, 1866, in New Brit-
      ain, Ct.

Authority. Mrs. Rebecca S. Peck (**53**). See also *Andrews'
New Britain.*

54.

William Whittlesey[7] (*Dan,*[6] *Matthew,*[5] *Dan,*[4] *John,*[3] *Matthew,*[2] *John*[1]), b. March 19. 1834, in Farmington, Ct., in that part of East Farms school district which was set off to the town of New Britain by the State Legislature of 1859. He removed in March, 1856, to Durant, Cedar Co., Iowa; married March 19, 1857, Mary Jane Stoddard, born April 30, 1834, daughter of Hiram Edwards and Fanny (Filley) Stoddard of Newington. Ct. He engaged in farming in Durant until Sept. 26, 1862, when he enlisted in the 6th Ohio Cavalry; was with Gen. Sully's command against the Indians in the North West, and was discharged Oct. 17, 1865. In April, 1866, he removed to Tell township, Boone Co., Iowa. He has held a great number of public offices in the township— trustee, clerk, justice of the peace, school director, secretary of the school board, and assessor, and is also a deacon in the church.

Children :

i.   MARY FRANCES. b. Jan. 12, 1858, in Durant, Iowa.
ii.   WILLIAM HUDSON. b. Aug. 27. 1860, in Durant, Iowa.
iii.   JOHN STODDARD, b. April 7, 1868, in Tell Township.
iv.   FANNY ELIZA, b. June 7, 1869. in Tell Township.
v.   ALVIN BURDETTE, b. Feb. 15, 1872. in Tell Township.
vi.   FRANKLIN DAVID. b. Aug. 14. 1876, in Tell Township.

Authority for above. William W. Clark (**54**). See also *Genealogy of Descendants of John Stoddard, **73**.*

55.

Elbert Cornelius[7] (*Dan,*[6] *Matthew,*[5] *Dan,*[4] *John,*[3] *Matthew,*[2] *John*[1]), b. July 30, 1838, in his father's house on Clark Hill. New Britain. Ct. : married Sept. 8, 1864, at Durant, Iowa, Ada Theresa Hitchcock. born Sept. 8, 1845, daughter of Jared B. and Lucy A. (Hubbard) Hitchcock. He removed to Boone Co. in the year 1868, and has been a farmer until the last five years, during which he has lived in Ogden, in the same county, as a carpenter.

Children:

i.   Anna Cornelia, b. Sept. 28, 1865, in Durant, Iowa.
ii. Ella Theresa, b. Feb. 3, 1869, in Boone Co., Iowa.
iii. Eugene Grant, b. March 31, 1871, in Boone Co., Iowa.
iv. Whittlesey Hubbard, b. Nov. 16, 1872, in Boone Co., Iowa.
v.   Josephine, b. Aug. 3, 1874, in Boone Co., Iowa.

Authority for above, Mrs. Rebecca S. Peck (**53**).

56.   HOLBROOK.

Frances Fedora[7] (*Dan,*[6] *Matthew,*[5] *Dan,*[4] *John,*[3] *Matthew,*[2] *John*[1]), b. March 15, 1841, in her father's house on Clark Hill, New Britain, Ct.; m. Feb. 2, 1875, Franklin Holbrook, born Nov. 30, 1809, at Townshend, Vt., son of Jared and Chloe (Dunton) Holbrook. Mr. Holbrook is a farmer, at Boonsboro, Iowa.

57.

Matthew Henry[7] (*Dan,*[6] *Matthew,*[5] *Dan,*[4] *John,*[3] *Matthew,*[2] *John*[1]), b. Aug. 8, 1846, at his father's house on Clark Hill, New Britain, Ct.: m. Sept. 15, 1874, Mary Epps, born April 11, 1858, daughter of John and Charlotte (Evans) Epps, of Grand Junction, Green Co., Iowa, and is a painter.

Children:

i.   Charles Edward, b. July 9, 1875.
ii. Frederic Dwight, b. April 11, 1878.

Authority, William W. Clark (**54**).

58.

Adrian Ives[7] (*Dan,*[6] *Matthew,*[5] *Dan,*[4] *John,*[3] *Matthew,*[2] *John*[1]), b. Sept. 15, 1849, in his father's house on Clark Hill,

11

New Britain, Ct.: m. Sept. 15, 1870, in Morris, Ct., Ascnath Whittlesey, born Feb. 25, 1849, daughter of David Waller and Dolly Betsey (Averell) Whittlesey. He lives in Boonsboro, Iowa, and is a painter.

Children:

i.   DAN WHITTLESEY, b. June 13, 1872 ; d. July 13, 1874.
ii. BESSIE AVERILL, b. Dec. 31, 1873 ; d. July 26, 1874.
iii. JAMES WHITTLESEY, b. May 28, 1876.
iv. DAVID, b. Feb. 15, 1878.

Authority, Mrs. Rebecca S. Peek (**53**).   See also *Memorial of the Whittlesey Family* (**51**).

59.

William Braddock (*Abel Newell,[5] John,[3] Abel,[4] John,[3] Matthew,[2] John[1]*), b. June 29, 1841 ; m. May 13, 1863, Caroline Hollister Robbins, born March 22, 1844, daughter of Philemon Frederick and Emily Strickland Robbins. Is Assistant Secretary of the Ætna Fire Insurance Co. of Hartford, Ct.

Children, all born in Hartford:

i.   WILLIAM ROBBINS, b. July 10, 1865 ; d. April 3, 1879.
ii. CHARLOTTE BRADDOCK, b. Jan. 10, 1868.
iii. ALICE ROBBINS, b. Jan. 21, 1870.
iv. FREDERICK WADSWORTH, b. Dec. 5, 1873 ; d. Aug. 8, 1875.

Authority, William B. Clark (**59**).

60.

Charles Leroy (*Abel Newell,[5] John,[3] Abel,[4] John, Matthew,[2] John[1]*), b. Feb. 11, 1843 ; m. Oct. 28, 1869, Cora A. Weatherly, born Oct. 25, 1848, in South Glastonbury, Ct., daughter of Charles S. and Frances H. Weatherly.

Children:

i. HARRY WEATHERLY, b. Oct. 19, 1870.
ii. FREDERIC BRADDOCK, b. Sept., 1872 ; d. Aug., 1874.

iii. CHARLES ARTHUR, b. Oct. 1, 1873.
iv. JOHN BRADDOCK, b. Oct., 1874.
v. LOUIS HERBERT, b. May 18, 1878.

Authority, William B. Clark (59).

62.

Charles Herbert (*James Webster,* *Sylvester,* *Abel,* *John,* *Matthew,* *John'*), b. Aug. 25, 1850, in Portsmouth. N. H.; m. Oct. 13, 1875, Emily Alice Woodworth of Hartford, born June 15, 1849, daughter of Mervin and Harriet Johnson Woodworth. Is in the office of the Charter Oak Insurance Co., Hartford, Ct.

Children:

i. ALEXANDER WOODWORTH, b. April 11, 1877, in Providence, R. I.
ii. CLEMENCE JOHNSON, b. Feb. 24, 1879, in Hartford, Ct.
iii. KATHARINE TAYLOR, b. Feb. 15, 1881, in Hartford, Ct.

63.   POTTER.

Annie Medora (*James Webster,* *Sylvester,* *Abel,* *John,* *Matthew,* *John'*), b. Sept. 4, 1852; m. April 12, 1875, F. J. Potter of Waterbury, Ct.

Children:

i. GRACE, b. Feb. 28, 1876.
ii. CHARLES HOWARD, b. Dec. 7, 1878.

INDEX.

ADAMS—
Alexander D., . 57
Charles E., 57
Edward, 57
Eliza J., . 56
James B., . 56
John, . 56
John C., 56
Maria S., . 57
Mark S., . 57
William H., 56
ALVORD—
Sarah, 47
ANDREWS—
Abraham, . 14
Benjamin, 25
Beulah, 47
Betsey, . 47
Catharine . 47
Catharine J., 54
Cornelia E., 54
Cynthia, 47
Elizabeth, 54
Jesse, 47
John C., . 54
Lydia, 46
Maria, 54
Mary, . 25
Mary A., . 54
Moses, 46, 54
Nancy, . 47
Noah, . 47
Sidney, 47, 54
BECKLEY—
Caroleen, . 73
Harriet, 73
Orin, 73

BELL—
John, 27
BIRD—
Esther, . 25
James, 13, 14
Joseph, . 13
Samuel, 25
BLISS—
Abigail, . 32
Peletiah, . 32
BOCKFORD—
Elnathan, . 11
BOUGHTON—
Sophronia, 45
BRADDOCK—
Emily L., . 71
John, . 71
BRITTAIN—
George S., 60
Henry, . 60
Mary L., . 60
BROWNSON—
Elizabeth, . 24
Samuel, . 24
Sarah, 24
BUCK—
Clarissa, 40
Isaac, 40
Prudence, . 40
BUCKINGHAM—
Gideon, 31
John, 31
Sarah, 31
BUNKER—
Eliphalet, . 47
BURNHAM—
Aaron R., . 54

BURNHAM—
  Aurilla,   54
  Silas,   54
CAMP—
  Phinehas, .   31
CASTLE—
  Eunice,   46
CATLIN—
  Dinah,   45
  James, .   45
  John, .   45
CHAMBERLIN—
  Rebecca, .   24
CHITTENDEN—
  John,   11
  William,   11
CLARK—
  Abel,   36, 43
  Abel N., .   55, 71
  Abi. 53
  Abigail,   18, 31, 32, 43, 53
  Abraham, . . 41, 49
  Adrian I., .   70, 81
  Alexander H., .   67
  Alexander W., .   83
  Alice R., .   82
  Almira,   60
  Alvin B., .   80
  Ann, .   31
  Anna C. . .   81
  Anne L., .   52
  Annie M. . .   74, 83
  Belle V.,   74
  Benoni, .   30
  Bessie A., .   82
  Caroleen B.,   74
  Charles A.,   83
  Charles E.,   81
  Charles H.,   74, 83
  Charles L.,   73, 82
  Charlotte, .   56, 74
  Charlotte B.,   82
  Clara E., . .   73
  Clemence J., . . . 83
  Dan, . 36, 42, 53, 69

CLARK—
  Dan W.,   . 82
  Daniel,   . 29
  David, .   33, 82
  Dennis W.,   52, 66
  Ebenezer, .   . 18
  Edward H.,   65, 73
  Elbert C., .   70, 80
  Eliza J., . . . 46, 56
  Elizabeth, . . 18, 23, 36, 46
  Elizur H., .   53
  Ella T., . . . 81
  Ellen A., .   55, 74
  Elnathan G.,   . 52
  Emma W.   . 67
  Eugene G.,   . 81
  Fanny E. . .   . 80
  Frances F.,   70, 81
  Franklin D.,   . 80
  Frederick B.,   82
  Frederick W., .   . 82
  George, .   53, 55
  George N. . . . 73
  Hannah, . 18, 29, 30, 31, 32
  Harry W , . . 82
  Henry, .   . 60
  Henry W.,   . 48, 58
  Huldah, . . 36, 41, 46, 52
  Isabella T.,   67
  James E. . . . 70
  James S. . . 53, 69, 70
  James W.,   56, 74, 82
  Jane,   36, 55, 56
  Jane A.,   . 56
  Jane E.,   52, 67
  Jane L. .   55
  Jared, .   31
  Jemima, . . 41
  John of Cambridge, . 5
  John of Farmington,   12
  John of Hartford, . . 8
  John of Saybrook, . . 10
  John, 18, 19, 23, 35, 36, 43, 46, 55
  John B., .   . 83
  John H., .   . 74

CLARK—
John S., . 80
John W.. . 55, 73
Jonathan, . . 31
Joseph, 11, 29, 37
Joseph F., . 65, 78
Joseph W.. 51, 52, 60
Josephine, 81
Julia A., . . 53
Katharine T . . . 83
Keziah, . 31
Langdon, . 56
Louis H., . 83
Lucy, . . 53
Lucy E., 52, 68
Lucy H., . . 65
Lucy S., 60
Lucila F., . 78
Manly, . 43, 53
Maria, . . 60, 75
Maria G., . . . 46, 57
Martha, . . 18, 30, 31
Mary, 18, 23, 27, 33, 34, 35, 43,
47, 52, 54
Mary A., . 69, 78
Mary E., 65, 73
Mary F., 80
Mary M., . 67
Mary P., . 55
Mary W.. . 52, 65
Matilda, . . 55, 70
Matthew, 18, 21, 23, 38, 43, 53
Matthew H., . . 70, 81
Mercy, . . 18, 35, 38
Mervin, 36, 40, 49, 59, 60, 75
Mervin W.. . 67
Moses, 29
Ophelia, . 56
Ornan, 41, 48
Rachel, . 18, 33
Rebecca, . 18, 25, 31
Rebecca S., . 70, 79
Ruth, 23, 36, 44
Samuel, . . 33, 43
Sarah, 18, 30, 37, 41, 48
Sylvester, . . . 44, 56
Thomas, . . . 30, 31

CLARK—
Thomas S., 60
Whittlesey H., . . . 81
William, . 29, 30
William B., 73, 82
William H., 64, 80
William R., . 82
William W.. 70, 80
CLINE—
Jacob L., . 52
COLLINS—
Lydia, . 27
COLTON—
Josiah, 34
Margaret, . 34
COOPER—
Jacob, 32
COWLES—
Nathaniel, 26
Phebe, 26
Sarah, 26
CURTISS—
Elizabeth, 33
John, . 33
Lydia, 33
DEMING—
Dan, . 55
DICKINSON—
Samuel, 20
Sukey, 20
DWYER—
David, 78
Ellen J., 78
Julia C., . 78
ELLSWORTH—
Elizabeth, 19, 24
Job, . . . 19
Josias, . 19, 24
Martha, 24
EPPS—
Charlotte, 81
John, 81
Mary, 81
EVEREST—
Abby, 74
Cornelius, 74
Cornelius B., 74

EVEREST—
  DeWitt C.,   74
  Nellie W.,   74
FESSENDEN—
  Jane W., .   60
  Joseph, .   61
  Sibbel L., .   61
FIELD—
  Martha,   54
  Robert, .   54
  Tirzah A.,   54
  Zachariah,   8
FLEMING—
  Ann M.,   40
  Mary T., .   40
  Samuel,   40
FLETCHER—
  Abigail, .   11
  Elizabeth, .   11
  Hannah,   11
  John,   11
  Mary,   11
  Rebecca,   11
  Samuel,   11
  Sarah,   11
FOWLER—
  Isaac,   32
  John,   32
  Mercy,   32
FRANCIS—
  Elijah,   36
  Hannah, .   36
  James,   47
  Romeo,   47
  Sylvia,   47
GAY—
  Fisher, .   75
  Florence T.,   75
  Julius, .   75
  Lucy, .   75
  Lucy C., .   75
  Mabel W.,   75
  Maria, .   75
GIBSON—
  Henry B.,   57
  Mary Y., .   57

GIDDINGS—
  Ruth,   53
  Sarah,   53
  Solomon, .   53
GILL—
  Elias,   . 65
  Elizabeth,   66
  Ellen,   65
  Emily,   65
  George,   65
  Jane,   65
  Mary,   . 65
  Samuel, .   . 65
  William W.,   66
GILLETT—
  Cornelia, .   52
  Cornelia M.,   52
  Eri, . .   52
  George F.,   52
  Hannah,   52
  Henry C.,   52
  Obadiah, .   52
GRAY—
  John,   45
  Mary,   45
GRIDLEY—
  Catharine,   52
  Dorothy, .   52
  Elizabeth,   25
  Jonathan,   25
  John,   24
  Mark,   . . 52
  Mary,   23, 24, 26
  Samuel,   23, 24, 26
  Thomas,   23, 24
GRISWOLD—
  Ezra,   47
  Lydia,   . 29
  Ruth,   . 47
  Samuel,   29
  Susanna,   29
GUPTIL—
  Caroline,   59
  John H., .   59
  Lucy,   59

HALL—
  Mary, 32
HAMLIN—
  Harriet, 52
  Lucy L., 52
  William, 52
HANUM—
  Elizabeth, . 32
HART—
  Asahel, 56
  Elizur, 53
  Hannah, . 56
  Sarah, 53
HAYDEN—
  Cicero M., 54
  Mary, . 54
  Susan P., . . 54
  Tirza, . . 44
HILLS—
  J. H., 47
HITCHCOCK—
  Ada T., . 80
  Jared B., . 80
  Lucy A., 80
HOLBROOK—
  Chloe, . 81
  Franklin, . 81
  Jared, . . 81
  John, 52
  John C., . 52
  Sarah, . 52
HOOKER—
  Lucy A., 60
  Octavia, . 60
  William, . 60
HOPKINS—
  Jeduthan, . 59
  Lucy, 59
  Matthew, . 59
HOTCHKISS—
  Ellen C., . 57
HOUGH—
  Abigail, 24
HOYT—
  Anne M., . 75
  Charlotte L., 75
  Eliza, . . . 75

HOYT—
  Elizabeth C., 75
  Franklin C., 75
  Frederic H., 75
  Jesse F., 75
  Lewis S., . 75
  Mary F., . . 75
HUBBS—
  Alexander, 66
  Mary, 66
  Mary C., 66
HUNTINGTON—
  Caleb, 29
  Ebenezer, . 29
  Elizabeth, . 29
  John, 29
  Mary, 29
  Rebecca, . 29
  Samuel, 27, 29
  Sarah, 11, 29
  Simon, 29
HUTTON—
  Gertrude, . 73
  Mancius H., 73
IVES—
  Abigail, 27
  Chauncey, 69
JONES—
  Caleb, 33
  Hezekiah, . 34
  Mary, 33, 34
  Samuel, 33
  Sylvanus, . 34
JUDD—
  Abigail, 43
  Benjamin, . 14
  Hannah, 24, 43
  James, 43
  John, 21
  Mary, 21
  Philip, 24
  Ruth, 21
  William, 24
KELLOGG—
  Jacob, 38
  Mary, . 38

12

LANGDON—
John, 23
Joseph, . 25
Sarah, . 25
Susanna, 26
LEE—
Lucy, 53
Martin, 53
Timothy, . 53
LEWIS—
Abi, . 42
Phinehas, . 42
Sarah, 42
William, . 13
LYMAN—
Anne, 40
Ebenezer, . 40
Laura, . 40
LYON—
Sarah, . 32
McCULLOUGH—
John, 44
McKINNEY—
Daniel, 45
Sally, 45
McKNIGHT—
John, 45
McKUNE—
Robert, 27
Sarah, 26
McNEIL—
Archibald, 38
Sarah, 38
MALLORY—
David S., . 79
James S., . 79
John S., . 79
Lucy, 79
Ransom, 79
MERRILL—
Isaac, 38
James, 38
Sarah, 38
METCALF—
Hannah, 29
Jonathan, . 29
Mehetebel, 29

NEWELL—
Elizabeth, 35
John, 35
NICHOLS—
Eunice, 40
NORTH—
Alvin, 49
Anna, 49
James, 53
Oren S., 48
Rhoda, 53
NORTON—
Hannah, 30
Thomas, 30
ORT—
John, 47
PARMALEE—
Mary, 37
PARSONS—
Hannah, 34
Miriam, 33
Samuel, 34
PEASE—
Abigail, 33
Mary, 33
Robert, 33
PECK—
Charles S., 79
Frederic W., 79
James G., 79
James S., . 79
Martha, . 79
Martha E., 79
Nehemiah, 79
PERCY—
Beulah, . 67
George W., 67
Josiah, . 67
PHELPS—
David, 34
Hannah, 34
Israel, 33
John, 34
Noah, 34
PIKE—
James, . 26

PINNEY—
Isaac, 25
Mary, 25
Sarah, 25
PIXLEY—
Abigail, 32
Clark, 32
David, 32
John, 32
Jonah, 32
Jonathan, . 32
Joseph, 32
Moses, 32
Sarah, 32
William, 32
PORTER—
Abigail, 26
Erastus, 20
Martha, . 26
Mary, . 26
Nathaniel, 26
Samuel, . 26
Shubael, . 20
Thomas, . 26
POTTER—
Charles H., 83
F. J., 83
Grace, 83
PRATT—
Elizabeth, . 11
William, 11
REED—
Irene, \ . 44
John, 44
Sally, 44
ROBBINS—
Caroline H., 82
Emily S., . 82
Philemon F., 82
ROGERS—
Abigail, . 54
Benjamin, 54
Charles E., 54
ROOT—
Eleazer, . 30
Experience, 30
Hannah, . 30

ROOT—
Joseph, 30
Martha, 30
Mary, . 30
Sarah, 30
Thomas, 30
ROSE—
Hannah, 30
ROWE—
Amanda, . 69
Isaiah, 69
Mary, 69
RUGGLES—
Ellen, 57
Henry J., . 57
Philo, 57
RUNYAN—
Elizabeth, 45
Sally, 45
Vincent, 45
RUSSELL—
Thomas, 47
SANFORD—
Edmund C., 68
Edmund P., 67
Martha, 67
Martha L., 68
Philo, 67
SERRELL—
Joseph, 68
Mary, 68
Rebecca, 68
SEXTON—
Deming W., 55
Nancy, 55
Walter, 55
SEYMOUR—
Lydia, . 38
Timothy, . 38
SHINN—
Anne H., . 69
Charles H., 69
Edwin, 69
Eli, . 68
Ellen M., . 69
Hannah B., 68
James, 68

SHINN—
  Joseph C.,   69
  Lucy E., .   69
  Mary A., .   68
  Milicent W.,   69
  Rebecca, .   68
  Thomas, .   68
  William H.,   68
SIBLEY—
  Emily W.,   57
  John C., .   57
  Mark H., .   57
  Mary H., .   57
SMITH—
  Catharine,   44
  Ephraim, .   26
  Heman,   34
  Henry,   44
  Ithamar,   34
  Joanna,   26
  Jonathan,   14
  Joseph,   26
  Lydia,   26
  Mary,   .   34
  Matthew, .   .   34
  Rachel,   .   26, 44
  Rebecca, .   .   34
  Ruth,   26, 34
  Samuel,   26, 34
  Sarah,   32
  Sibyl,   34
  Stephen, .   34
  Temperance.   .   44
  William,   13, 26
STANLEY—
  Asa, .   44
  Caleb W.,   45
  Cruger,   .   44
  Cyrus,   .   58
  Elizabeth,   45
  Emily W.,   58
  Erastus, .   44
  Horatio,   44
  Huldah,   45
  Jesse,   48
  John,   11
  Jonathan,   45

STANLEY—
  Katy,   44
  Lucius,   .   45
  Lucy,   .   42
  Lydia,   .   48
  Mary,   .   42
  Nancy,   44
  Noah,   .   44
  Ruth,   44, 45
  Salina,   .   44
  Seth,   44, 45
  Thomas,   42
  Timothy, .   48
STEELE—
  John,   13
STODDARD—
  Fanny,   80
  Hiram E., .   80
  Mary J.,   80
STREET—
  Nehemiah,   42
SWEET—
  Anna,   20
  John,   20
THARP—
  Amariah, .   59
  Elizabeth, .   59
  Mary J.,   59
TICHENOR—
  Eunice,   65
  Henry B., .   65
  Nehemiah,   65
TREAT—
  Abigail,   31
  Jonathan, .   31
  Robert,   .   31
VARRELL—
  Hall, .   74
  Mary, E., .   74
  N. M., .   74
WADSWORTH—
  Adrian R.,   79
  Decius, .   39
  Elizabeth, .   79
  George,   40
  Romeo,   40
  Ruth,   39

WADSWORTH—
Sidney, . 40
Thomas H., 79
William, . 39
William R., 40
WALKER—
Caleb, . 37, 46
Caleb R., . . 46
Elizabeth, . 37, 46
William, . 37
WALLACE—
John, 47
WARD—
Anthony, . 11
Edward, . 11
John, 11
Joyce, 11
Mary, 11
Robert, . 11
William, . 11
WARNER—
Andrew, 7, 11
Betsey, . 70
Charles A., 70
Elizabeth, . 19
Robert, 19
Sarah, 19
Willard, . 70
William A., 70
WASHBURN—
Joseph, 49
Milicent, 49
Ruth, 49
WATKINSON—
Elizabeth, . 65
Jane, . 65
William, 65
WEBSTER—
Fanny, . 74
Frances B., 74
William, . 74
WELCH—
Sally, 44
WETHERLY—
Charles S., 82
Cora A., . 82
Frances H., 82

WHAPLES—
Elizur, 38
Jonathan, . 38
Margaret, . 38
WHEDON—
Calvin, 45
Polly, 45
WHITE—
Joseph, 48
Lucy, 48
WHITMORE—
Lois, . . 44
WHITTLESEY—
Asenath, . 82
Betsey, . 82
David, . 69
David W., 82
Mary, 69
Rebecca, . 69
WIARD—
Eunice, 27
John, 27
Phebe, 27
WILCOX—
John, 9
WILSON—
Robert, 13
WINSHIP—
Edward, 6
WOODFORD—
Joseph, 33
Lydia, 33
Sarah, 33
WOODRUFF—
Abigail, 27
Abraham, . 40
Amos, 37
Daniel, 26
David, . 26
Ebenezer, . . 26
Hannah, 25, 33
Hezekiah, . . 26
John, . 27, 32
Jonathan, . 25
Joseph, . 32
Joshua, 55
Josiah, 33

WOODRUFF—

Mary,	36	Rebecca,	26
Matthew, .	25	Rede,	27
Prudence, .	55	Robert,	36
Rachel, . . . 27		WOODWORTH—	
Ruth, . . 26, 36, 38		· Emily A...	83
Samuel,	25, 36	Harriet J..	82
Sarah,	37, 40	Mervin,	83
Seth, .	37		

WOODRUFF—